iTEAM

Putting the "I" Back into Team

Also Available from Dorset House Publishing

iTEAM

Putting the "I" Back into Team

William E. Perry

DORSET HOUSE PUBLISHING
3143 BROADWAY, SUITE 2B
NEW YORK, NEW YORK 10027

Library of Congress Cataloging-in-Publication Data

Perry, William E.
  Iteam : putting the "I" back into team / William E. Perry.
      p. cm.
  Includes index.
  ISBN 978-0-932633-68-2 (alk. paper)
  1. Teams in the workplace. I. Title.
  HD66.P428 2009
  658.4'022--dc22

                                    2009017916

Quantity discounts are available from the publisher. Call (800) 342-6657 or (212) 620-4053 or e-mail info@dorsethouse.com. Contact same for examination copy requirements and permissions. To photocopy passages for academic use, obtain permission from the Copyright Clearance Center: (978) 750-8400 or www.copy right.com.

Trademark credits: All trade and product names are either trademarks, registered trademarks, or service marks of their respective companies, and are the property of their respective holders and should be treated as such.

Cover design by Claire Veligdan, Dorset House Publishing
Front cover image by Liv Friis-Larsen, ©iStockphoto.com/Team Effort
Author photograph courtesy of Life Touch Church Directories and Portraits

Distributed in the UK and EEC by Computer Bookshops Ltd., based in Birmingham, England (computerbookshops.com); in the English language in Singapore, the Philippines, and Southeast Asia by Alkem Company (S) Pte. Ltd., Singapore; and in the English language in India, Bangladesh, Sri Lanka, Nepal, and Mauritius by Prism Books Pvt., Ltd., Bangalore, India.

Printed in the United States of America

Library of Congress Catalog Number: 2009017916

ISBN: 978-0-932633-68-2

12 11 10 9 8 7 6 5 4 3 2 1

Dedication

To both
those sadly lacking team leaders who showed me
how not to run a team
and
those outstanding team leaders who taught me
how to effectively run teams to accomplish well-defined goals

Contents

Acknowledgments xi

Foreword xiii

1　Reengineering the Team Approach
　　to Problem Solving 3
　　Team Approaches That Contribute to Success and Failure 4
　　The Business Team's Cast of Characters................................6
　　Four Types of Business Teams 7
　　Team-Effectiveness Self-Assessment....................................8
　　　　Workpaper #1: Team-Effectiveness Self-Assessment 10
　　　　Analysis Results 15
　　Four Principles That Make Great Teams Great...................................16
　　　　Score Analysis 17

2　The Top-Ten Challenges
　　to Effective Teamwork 19
　　"Laws" That Inhibit Team Success 20
　　How the Top-Ten Challenges Were Identified 22
　　　　Interrelationships Between Challenges 23

3　Challenge 1: Selecting a Team Leader
　　Who Will Lead 25
　　Putting the "I" into Selecting a Team Leader Who Will Lead 25
　　Typical Approach to Selecting a Team Leader 26
　　World-Class Approach to Selecting a Team Leader................................26
　　Five Selecting-a-Team-Leader Best Team Practices 27
　　Impediments to the Team-Leader Challenge 31

Strategies to Overcome the Team-Leader Challenge 32
Team-Leader Plan of Action 32

4 Challenge 2: Defining Team Entrance and Exit Criteria 34

Putting the "I" into Defining Team Entrance and Exit Criteria 35
Typical Approach to Defining Entrance and Exit Criteria 36
World-Class Approach to Defining Entrance and Exit Criteria 36
Five Defining-Entrance-and-Exit-Criteria Best Team Practices 37
Impediments to the Defining-Entrance-and-
    Exit-Criteria Challenge 43
Strategies to Overcome the Defining-Entrance-and-
    Exit-Criteria Challenge 44
Entrance-and-Exit-Criteria Plan of Action 45

5 Challenge 3: Selecting Team Members for Specific Roles 47

Putting the "I" into Selecting Team Members 48
Typical Approach to Selecting Team Members 49
World-Class Approach to Selecting Team Members 50
Five Team-Member-Selection Best Team Practices 51
Impediments to the Team-Member-Selection Challenge 55
Strategies to Overcome the Team-Member-Selection Challenge 56
Team-Member-Selection Plan of Action 57

6 Challenge 4: Building Trust Among Team Members 58

Putting the "I" into Building Trust Among Team Members 59
Typical Approach to Building Trust Among Team Members 59
World-Class Approach to Building Trust Among Team Members 60
Five Building-Team-Trust Best Team Practices 61
Impediments to the Building-Team-Trust Challenge 65
Strategies to Overcome the Building-Team-Trust Challenge 65
Building-Team-Trust Plan of Action 66

7 Challenge 5: Training Team Members to Accomplish Their Assignments 67

Putting the "I" into Training Team Members 68
Typical Approach to Training Team Members 69
World-Class Approach to Training Team Members 69
Five Training-Team-Members Best Team Practices 69

Impediments to the Training-Team-Members Challenge 74
Strategies to Overcome the Training-Team-Members Challenge............76
Training-Team-Members Plan of Action 76

8 Challenge 6: Listening to the Voice of the Customer 78

Putting the "I" into Listening to the Voice of the Customer................79
Typical Approach to Listening to the Voice of the Customer...............79
World-Class Approach to Listening to the Voice of the Customer.............80
Five Voice-of-the-Customer Best Team Practices 82
Impediments to the Voice-of-the-Customer Challenge.......................85
Strategies to Overcome the Voice-of-the-Customer Challenge 86
Voice-of-the-Customer Plan of Action..86

9 Challenge 7: Breaking Down Silos............................88

Putting the "I" into Breaking Down Silos..89
Typical Approach to Breaking Down Silos 90
World-Class Approach to Breaking Down Silos..................................90
Five Breaking-Down-Silos Best Team Practices 91
Impediments to the Breaking-Down-Silos Challenge..........................94
Strategies to Overcome the Breaking-Down-Silos Challenge 95
Breaking-Down-Silos Plan of Action 96

10 Challenge 8: Avoiding Groupthink............................97

Putting the "I" into Avoiding Groupthink 98
Typical Approach to Avoiding Groupthink 99
World-Class Approach to Avoiding Groupthink...................................99
Five Groupthink-Avoidance Best Team Practices 100
Impediments to the Groupthink-Avoidance Challenge.......................103
Strategies to Overcome the Groupthink-Avoidance Challenge 104
Groupthink-Avoidance Plan of Action 105

11 Challenge 9: Assuring That Team Efforts Are Successful 106

Putting the "I" into Assuring Team Success 107
Typical Approach to Assuring Team Success 107
World-Class Approach to Assuring Team Success 108
Five Assuring-Team-Success Best Team Practices 109
Impediments to the Assuring-Team-Success Challenge.......................112
Strategies to Overcome the Team-Success Challenge 113
Assuring-Team-Success Plan of Action 114

**12   Challenge 10: Rewarding Individual
      Team Members** **115**
      Putting the "I" into Rewarding Individual Team Members 116
      Typical Approach to Rewarding Individual Team Members 116
      World-Class Approach to Rewarding Individual Team Members...........117
      Five Individual-Team-Member-Rewards Best Team Practices............118
      Impediments to the Individual-Team-Member-
           Rewards Challenge 121
      Strategies to Overcome the Individual-Team-Member-
           Rewards Challenge 122
      Individual-Team-Member-Rewards Plan of Action 123

**13   The Ultimate Team Challenge:
      Keeping Teamwork Competitive**..............................**125**
      Keeping Teamwork Competitive Is As Simple As 1, 2, 3 126
           Step 1: Establish your baseline of team performance. 126
           Step 2: Define your teamwork goal. 127
           Step 3: Develop a plan to move from your baseline to your goal. 127
      Emerging Team Practices 127
      Final Thoughts on Putting the "I" Back into Team............................131

Index **133**

Acknowledgments

I have been fascinated over the years by how a change in owner-ship or management can make or break an established business. The book you are about to read tells many tales of ways individ-uals—as team leaders and team members—can and should influ-ence teams to achieve success. The book, itself, is my acknowledg-ment of so many role models in business and in sports from whose actions I have learned.

I have learned as well from businesses destroyed by a change made by those responsible for running them, and it is what can be learned from failure that I choose to acknowledge now. Take, for example, one very successful boutique not far from our home in Orlando where my wife and her friends loved to shop. Business was booming when the shop was bought by new owners, possibly young MBAs who thought they knew more about the business than the previous owners had known. Before long, they had changed almost everything. Sadly, the shop failed, closing its doors within a year.

Or, consider the experience of new owners who bought my good friend Philip Crosby's "Quality Is Free" software-defects-analysis business and soon thereafter decided that Philip's input was no longer needed. For all intents and purposes, the new owners destroyed a thriving business within a few years.

In flagging failure in the stories of these unnamed owners and managers, I hope to communicate my strong conviction that from bad good can come. In writing this book, I have drawn on lessons learned, particularly from very good and very bad team leaders. And I have discovered that team leaders are no different than new business owners. If they believe they can make positive change without the benefit of history and the insight of team members and stakeholders, they are as doomed to fail as the folks who ran the dress shop into the ground and the company that destroyed Philip Crosby's quality-related business.

My goal in this book is to capture best team practices, and to emphasize techniques and actions that will help team leaders and team members make good teams better and better teams great. To you, I raise my acknowledgments' glass.

One final set of acknowledgments is in order: In the course of writing this book, I have followed my own advice and listened to and learned from the best. I am indebted to Karis Holnagel of Quality Assurance Institute for her patience in assembling the many parts of my manuscript. I am grateful as well to the editorial team at Dorset House, where Claire Veligdan, Wendy Eakin, and their colleagues have taken what I hoped would be a good book and made it, dare I say, great. Thank you, all.

Foreword

The four stages in the life cycle of a butterfly—egg, larval, pupa, and adult—illustrate ways readers can use the information in this book. The egg stage comes first, and for a team, it centers on forming and solidifying the boundaries of the team's work—activities that are key to the team's survival and success. Next comes the larval caterpillar stage, during which the analogous teams take in data and instructions (akin to the caterpillar larva as it eats, taking in nourishment seemingly nonstop). During this stage, the team takes in information to prepare for beginning work on a project. The third stage is the pupa, when a caterpillar seeks out the optimal habitat for chrysalis, in preparation for its transforming into a butterfly through metamorphosis. The fourth stage is the adult stage when metamorphosis has transformed the caterpillar into a butterfly, but during which the adult finishes growing and now uses its new body. This is the stage at which a team assembles its work into a finished product.

My point with this analogy is to make vivid how effective teams should work through a transformation process. The first stage involves solidifying team members and goals. The second stage involves learning; the third, planning; the fourth, doing. If team members are open to a process similar to what a caterpillar undergoes to become a butterfly, they will be well on their way to accomplishing their mission. This calls for performing three simple steps:

- Step 1: *Learn* the material in the book.
- Step 2: *Plan* the actions to take.
- Step 3: *Do* what's planned.

In Step 1, think first of the work of the hundreds of team members who contributed the material, all of which represents how effective teams operate. Be cognizant of the probability that failing to do the things that successful teams do can result in limited success for a team—or worse. Learn the material by reading the book front to back, as if reading a novel. Be certain to understand the reasons for overcoming the challenges, and analyze how the accompanying building blocks and best team practices will facilitate a team's overcoming the challenges.

In Step 2, begin by thinking about possible consequences of working without a plan. Stated to sound the alarm: If a team fails to plan, it can plan to fail. Beginning a meeting by brainstorming is not as effective as first determining a road map for how the team will accomplish its mission and then employing brainstorming to work out the details. You know what challenges your organization has already overcome, but be proactive and think ahead to those it will need to address in its team methodology. Using the material in this book, build a plan that will enable a single, specific team to operate effectively and establish team procedures that will enable all teams to be effective.

In Step 3, internalize the idea that a plan once developed is a moral, if not legal, contract between a team and project stake-holders who have a vested interest in what the team is trying to accomplish. If a team agrees to a plan with stakeholders, it is the team's responsibility to execute that plan. If conditions change, the plan needs to change—once the modified plan has support, execute the modified plan.

That's it! Now you are ready to absorb the ideas and information in this book, and then use them to move your teams to world-class status.

April 2009   W.E.P.
Orlando, Florida

iTEAM

Putting the "I" Back into Team

1

Reengineering the Team Approach to Problem Solving

Most of us have a love-hate relationship with teams. We love sports teams, for example—*Yea! Go Team!*—but few of us genuinely enjoy having to participate in team activities at work. Although I have had the best of times as a member of a team that accomplished much more than the sum of each person's input, I've also had the worst of times as a team member, when a poor group dynamic actually diminished team-member contributions.

I have concluded, after thousands of hours sitting through team meetings, that there are very, very few *great* teams. I am convinced, however, that great teams can and do exist, and that it is possible to transform a good team into a great team.

The reason we need to make the effort is that teams are becoming increasingly important in today's business culture, and the use of teams to solve business problems will increase in the future. Decisions now made by management will more and more frequently be made and implemented by teams. Teams enable organizations to readily capture the creativity and innovative methods of individuals in an organization. The reality, however, is that, in many business organizations, teams are completely ineffective.

As evidence of a flawed team theory, signs adorn many IT departments and work stations, stating, "There is no 'I' in 'team.'" The message is clear, leaving individuals to ask, "If there is no 'I' in 'team,' what am *I* supposed to do during team meetings? Do *I* have a role? Will *I* receive recognition for my work and earn reward based on that work? Am *I* to contribute as an individual or am I just part of a groupthink, mob-mentality exercise?"

Having spent more than ten-thousand, frequently boring hours in meetings, I find myself fascinated with the topic of effectiveness and teams. I certainly have put in sufficient time to claim some sort of expertise on the subject. In fact, for my servitude, I was awarded a CMMM certificate, recognizing me as Certified Master Meeting Member.

Through team-participation experience and interviews with hundreds of individuals who have spent hundreds of thousands of hours in team meetings, I have learned to recognize the attributes of *great* teams and great teamwork. I have learned that great teams are not born; they are built.

This book treats what I believe are the top-ten challenges facing teams and contains fifty building blocks, called "best team practices," that anyone can use in the drive to build a great, world-class team. The fifty building blocks are phrased as questions to suggest solutions for battling the challenges teams face on their journey to becoming great.

In this introductory chapter, you will encounter topics such as the following that are central to discussions throughout the book:

1. teamwork approaches that lead to team success and failure
2. various personalities and skills of the business-team's cast of characters
3. four types of business teams
4. team-effectiveness self-assessment challenges and questionnaire
5. four principles that make a team great

Team Approaches That Contribute to Success and Failure

Many organizations develop a detrimental step-by-step approach such as the following for tackling business-team tasks:[1]

- Step 1: Identify a task that management doesn't want to perform.

---

[1]In this book, I use the term "business team" to describe any team other than a sports team.

- Step 2: Assign people who both should care about accomplishing the specific task and who have no valid excuse for not being on a business team addressing the problem.
- Step 3: Instruct team members to discuss all aspects of the problem *in depth* regardless of whether they are relevant to solving the problem.
- Step 4: Continue discussions ad nauseam until groupthink takes hold or team members rebel, just plain tired of meeting.
- Step 5: Recommend a problem solution, even if team members have no idea how effective it will be, to end the agony of team meetings.

Let's use a sports analogy to see how well this common business-team approach would work: Imagine that your task is to form a Little League baseball team whose first game will be against a long-established team named the League-Leader Yankees—a team known to employ proven, winning practices. With more than a touch of irony, you name your start-up team the Cellar Dwellers, and set out to find a team manager. The best candidate is a go-get-'em father who wants his kids to play baseball (even though they do not appear to be in the least bit enthusiastic), and so you appoint him team manager. Without conducting tryouts, your new team manager puts his kids and his friends' kids on the team, encouraging each father to lobby for the position he wants his kid to play. "Strategic planning" consists of discussing how much time each kid will play the position his or her dad has chosen. With no structured practice and little direction, the Cellar Dwellers unsurprisingly lose their first game and every game thereafter, ending in last place at the end of the season.

Now imagine how the League-Leader Yankees approach team activities at the start of each season. First, they recruit a manager with baseball-coaching experience who has proven he can win. The manager organizes a camp to test players for each position, and then recruits the best players to join his team. Players practice their positions and improve their skills. The manager develops a game plan and motivates individuals to play their position to the best of their ability. The manager states first that he is 100-percent responsible for game outcome, whether the team wins or loses, and second, that the team members are responsible for playing their position as instructed. It should be no surprise that the League-Leader Yankees win the championship once again.

So, if selecting the best people, planning strategically, practicing skill sets, and giving individuals responsibility for "playing their position" can help sports teams to succeed, shouldn't we try to apply this approach to achieve business-team success? The answer is a simple yes. Getting all components to work is not simple, however, generally because business-team members erroneously believe "there is no 'I' in team."

In professional sports, there *is* an "I" in team. Each team member knows his or her role, pursues well-defined objectives, trains to fulfill specific responsibilities, and earns reward for individual performance—regardless of team results. It is fact that professional-sports players on losing teams can earn recognition and reward if they have performed well as individuals, but if a professional sports team continually loses, the owners are almost guaranteed to fire the manager—they may also opt to trade players or refuse to renew contracts. In business, team members are much more likely to be punished than their managers if a team fails to perform.

The Business Team's Cast of Characters

It is easy to visualize the members of a Little League team—a pitcher, a catcher, a first baseman, and so forth. Now try to picture the members of an IT business team—you might come up with a project leader, systems analysts, testers, and so on, but that's not the cast of characters I began to identify during my more than ten-thousand hours of team meetings. My business-meeting cast of characters includes the following:

- *Dominator:* An individual who tries to take charge of meetings, control their direction, and impose his or her solutions upon other team members.
- *Talker:* Someone with thoughts on everything, particularly on topics irrelevant to the problem at hand.
- *Bystander:* An individual who does not want to attend, participate, or contribute anything to the meeting, who

escapes into his or her own world, completely mentally withdrawing from the meeting.

- *Volunteer:* An individual who can't wait to serve on a team, perform whatever specific tasks need doing, and handle meeting administrivia.
- *My-Way Commander:* An individual who always claims to know *the only correct way* to solve the problem.
- *Escalator:* An individual who escalates a solvable problem by epic proportions into a problem impossible to solve.
- *Detailer:* An individual who reduces discussion into minute subtopics to be resolved prior to identifying the problem to be solved.
- *Destroyer:* An individual with a hidden agenda, which usually differs from the problem at hand, who is especially dangerous because he or she may publicly agree with the team but work against its goals.
- *Intimidator:* An individual who tries to take over meetings by overstating his or her importance.

Teams made up of people with some or all of these characteristics sometimes may be successful, but they are generally ineffective. Although I typically will not reference these characters in future chapters, you may find yourself recalling them, bringing them to life as the book addresses the challenges in developing great teams.

Four Types of Business Teams

Teams frequently pursue operating objectives that stand in the way of their being or becoming great teams, pursuing goals either that conflict with the overall business's objectives or that do little or nothing to move the business toward accomplishing those objectives. Operating objectives determine a team's results—most teams understand this as fact, but their objectives place them in one of three less-than-stellar categories. Alone in the fourth category are teams that can be considered world-class.

During my years as a team member and manager, I've found that most business teams, when considered in terms of their essentials, function as one of four basic types:

- *Show and Tell:* These teams have no objective and no stated goals to accomplish. They generate documents and lists without solving a problem, and then they describe their actions. Participants do just two things: First, they "show" what they have done since the previous meeting; second, they "tell" what they plan to do until the next meeting.
- *Tell and Go:* These teams are dictatorships. Instead of being encouraged to contribute their best input and work, team members are told exactly what to do—with no opportunity for discussion. Managers "tell" individual team members what they want them to do, and then team members "go" off and do it.
- *Search and Seize:* These teams' members "search" for alternatives to solve the problem at hand and then "seize" a solution to end the agony of teamwork.
- *World-Class:* These teams consist of members who do what is right for the organization, do what is right the right way, and earn rewards for success.

There are exceptions, of course, with some teams functioning as a mix of types, but it is safe to report that teams having characteristics of the first three types usually produce mediocre or worthless results. Teams whose members possess good work ethics and determination generally can grow into world-class teams, a goal every team should set its sights on.

Team–Effectiveness Self–Assessment

Most people have participated on some form of sports team while in school, and almost everyone has experienced team dynamics outside of sports, be it in a classroom situation, as a family member, or in a business organization. Think for some moments about your own experiences with business teams performing activities other than sports, focusing in particular on the effectiveness of those teams versus how effective they might have been had they operated up to their full potential—in other words, if they had been "world-class" business teams. Keeping one specific team experience in mind—the focal team—complete the self-assessment questionnaire in Workpaper #1, on the following pages, which introduces the top-ten team challenges and prods your examination by means of fifty questions that pertain to properties associated with great teams. Some entries may not make complete sense to you on this first attempt, but each will be fully explored in chapters to come.

To answer questions about team practices, consider the focal team's success in terms of the following:

- *Fully Effective:* A checkmark here confirms a business team that uses the practice identified in the question, effectively enabling the team to accomplish its assigned mission.
- *Partially Effective:* Checking this entry indicates that the practice is either implemented partially, or is fully implemented but is only used occasionally.
- *Not Effective:* A checkmark here indicates a team that did not use the practice identified in the question or, if used, the practice did not contribute to the team's ability to accomplish its mission.

If you are not familiar with a specific practice, assess that practice as Not Effective and then move on to the next entry. Although material in this book will explain each of the practices, do not skip ahead to the applicable chapter before completing Workpaper #1, and *do not* read the Analysis Results and Score Analysis sections before completing the self-assessment, as doing so may affect the veracity of your responses.

WORKPAPER #1:
Team–Effectiveness Self–Assessment

Challenge 1: Selecting a team leader who will lead	Fully Effective	Partially Effective	Not Effective
• Does the team leader have experience as a successful team leader?			
• Is the team leader solely responsible for the success of the team?			
• Is the team leader the primary decision-maker for the team?			
• Does the team leader coach team members in how to best fulfill their team responsibilities?			
• Does the team leader encourage and motivate team members to fulfill their team responsibilities?			
SCORE FOR CHALLENGE 1:			

Challenge 2: Defining entrance and exit criteria			
• Are the entrance criteria met before team activities commence?			
• Is the team provided with exit criteria before commencing team activities?			
• Does the organization establish procedures for the team to follow to perform team assignments?			
• Is a specific team member (for example, a team judge) responsible for ruling whether or not specific discussions continue and/or specific team activities occur?			
• Are individuals prepared to be productive team members?			
SCORE FOR CHALLENGE 2:			

Challenge 3: Selecting team members to fulfill specific roles	Fully Effective	Partially Effective	Not Effective
• Does the team leader define the team composition required to achieve exit criteria?			
• Does the team-member selection process include identifying the most desirable individuals to fulfill each team role?			
• Does the team leader recruit team members to fulfill defined team roles, rather than appointing or selecting team members based on outside factors?			
• Does the team leader provide training or supplement missing skills for recruited team members?			
• Does the team leader identify back-up aids for each team member in case a team member cannot fulfill his or her role?			
SCORE FOR CHALLENGE 3:			

Challenge 4: Building trust among team members			
• Does the team have—and do team members sign—a team Code of Ethics?			
• Does the team leader exhibit the attitudes and actions he or she wants team members to emulate (that is, walk the talk)?			
• Does the team leader first select an assistant team leader he or she explicitly trusts?			
• Does the team leader reward individual failure, even failure due to incompetence?			
• Does the team leader select the right team members (that is, people with personal chemistry) instead of selecting the best-skilled team members who may or may not have worked well together?			
SCORE FOR CHALLENGE 4:			

Challenge 5: Training team members to accomplish their assignments	Fully Effective	Partially Effective	Not Effective
• Does the team differentiate between team success and individual success?			
• Does the team leader objectively define assignments for team members?			
• Does the team leader develop a training plan for each team member?			
• Do team members share the philosophy not to let any individual team member fail?			
• Did the team leader appoint a quality-control coach for the team?			
SCORE FOR CHALLENGE 5:			

Challenge 6: Listening to the voice of the customer			
• Does the team know customers' acceptance criteria?			
• Does the team plan to survey customers before, during, and after completion of team activities?			
• Do team members visit customers' sites and observe their work firsthand?			
• Does the team invite customers to participate in focus groups, to independently work with facilitators to evaluate proposals and/or products, and to define their needs and assess the team's activities?			
• Does the team ask customers to participate in team activities to voice their needs?			
SCORE FOR CHALLENGE 6:			

Challenge 7: Breaking down silos	Fully Effective	Partially Effective	Not Effective
• Does the team include supportive individuals from departments that could impede its mission?			
• Does the team diagram how organizational units whose cooperation is necessary to accomplish the team mission really work?			
• Could the team push the limits of its authority if necessary?			
• Does the team collect and present statistics about processes it could leverage to gain other departments' support for its mission?			
• Did the team clearly define "what's in it for me" for each stakeholder involved in implementing changes needed to accomplish the team's mission?			
SCORE FOR CHALLENGE 7:			

Challenge 8: Avoiding groupthink			
• Does the team define a method for making team decisions?			
• Does the team ensure adequate representation of dissenting positions by inviting adversaries to join the team?			
• Does the team vote secretly on recommendations, particularly final recommendations?			
• Do team members ensure their conclusions are not subject to groupthink by using an anti-groupthink checklist?			
• Do individual members conduct periodic team-performance evaluations?			
SCORE FOR CHALLENGE 8:			

Challenge 9: Assuring that team efforts are successful	Fully Effective	Partially Effective	Not Effective
• Does the team make sure the organization could actually implement its recommendations?			
• Does the team determine that stakeholders are aligned with the team objective?			
• Does the team ensure that appropriate levels of management will actively work toward its success?			
• Does the team determine whether its project goals are right for the business?			
• Does the team leader assure that team members commit to successfully implementing their recommendations before making them?			
SCORE FOR CHALLENGE 9:			

Challenge 10: Rewarding individual team members			
• Does the team leader determine what type of rewards would motivate each team member?			
• Are rewards public, and criticism private?			
• Did the team identify and reward team-member innovation?			
• Can team members help ascertain each other's contributions?			
• Does the team leader recognize and reward clerical support personnel?			
SCORE FOR CHALLENGE 10:			

TOTAL SCORE FOR *ALL 10* CHALLENGES:

Analysis Results

Your self-assessment effort enables you to analyze your focal team's effectiveness, but its real value is to identify areas and strategies for improvement in existing and future teams. Calculate the score for each category from the self-assessment as follows:

- For each practice that you check "Fully Effective," allocate two points.
- For each practice that you check "Partially Effective," allocate one point.
- For each practice that you check "Not Effective," mark the score as zero.
- At the end of each of the team challenges, calculate the total number of points.

The results for each challenge will range from 0 to 10. Tally the score for each challenge as well as the total score. The total score, between 0 and 100, indicates the effectiveness of the focal team's overall approach to teamwork. Next, analyze your responses, challenge by challenge. This analysis will determine how effective the focal team is at addressing each of the top-ten challenges. Post the score for each challenge on a footprint chart (see Figure 1). To create the chart, draw a set of five concentric circles, labeled with even numbers 2 to 10. Then, write numbers 1 through 10 at equidistant points along the circumference of the outermost circle to correspond to each of the top ten challenges.

Next, shoot an invisible ray from your "1" to mark a dot in the concentric circle whose number matches the score for Challenge 1. Repeat this process until you have marked a score-dot to represent the focal team's score for each of the ten challenges. When you've marked all ten challenge score-dots, connect the score-dots, beginning with the first you marked, connecting in sequence until you reach the tenth score-dot. Then, connect the tenth score-dot to the first dot to close the footprint. This is your Footprint Chart, which indicates the effectiveness of the focal team. Use this visual to help pinpoint current team strengths and weaknesses and to guide future teams aspiring to greatness.

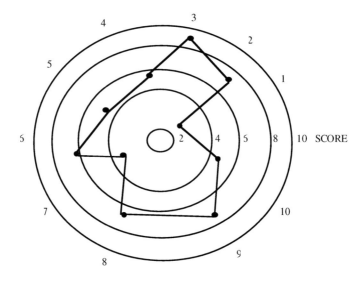

Figure 1.1: Team Effectiveness Footprint Chart.

As an example, in the figure, I've marked the first score-dot, indicating a score of 3 for my hypothetical focal team's effectiveness in meeting Challenge 1, and so forth, for each challenge. After considering your focal team's effectiveness in addressing each of the top-ten challenges, use the Footprint Chart and the total score for the ten challenges to analyze total team effectiveness. Now read through the Score Analysis section on the facing page to analyze your focal team's total effectiveness.

Four Principles That Make Great Teams Great

Understanding and investing in the following principles will help individuals address and resolve challenges to team effectiveness:

- *Team-Effectiveness Principle 1:* Successful business organizations are not democracies.
- *Team-Effectiveness Principle 2:* Business organizations have a mission to accomplish. Everything a business does should focus on accomplishing its mission. Other tasks

(continued on page 18)

Score Analysis

81-100 points
The team has a world-class approach to team effectiveness, and undoubtedly is very effective in accomplishing assigned missions. Team members make a valuable contribution to accomplishing missions and earn reward for their efforts. However, if there are any areas for which the team scored a 0, improvement in those areas provides the team with an opportunity to go from great to super-great.

61-80 points
The team usually accomplishes missions. However, team or organizational culture may de-motivate individuals, minimizing their contributions to team success. The team should carefully analyze those practices that were scored 0 or 1 and develop a plan to improve the organization's approach to teamwork, effectiveness, and efficiency.

41-60 points
The team functions like the majority of business teams and indicates that the organization develops teams similar to the way many other business organizations develop teams. Most likely, some team members do not contribute, and the team is susceptible to a few individuals dominating team activities. The organization has adequate practices in place so that, with minimal effort, it can significantly improve team effectiveness. The results of the self-assessment identify areas for improvement.

21-40 points
The team does not perform well. Lack of world-class team practices probably causes dissatisfaction among team members. Individuals in the organization probably do not want to be assigned to a team and do not believe teams are an effective way to resolve issues or to complete tasks. One or two people dominate a team and the rest go along regardless of whether they believe in the solution. The organization requires an extensive effort to develop effective teams.

0-20 points
The team is nonfunctional. The organization wastes resources building and using teams to solve business problems. Individuals have no incentive to work on team activities. If management wants to use teams to solve business problems, it needs to develop best practices in all ten challenge areas.

waste resources and will limit the ability of a business organization to accomplish its mission.

- *Team-Effectiveness Principle 3:* Teams should not be democracies. Teams, like business organizations, should operate as monarchies. Just as a CEO should not call for a vote on what a business organization should do, a team leader should not call for a vote on what the team should do. (Note: This principle does not mean consensus is unimportant but rather that team leaders must do what they believe is right regardless of potential opposition from team members.)
- *Team-Effectiveness Principle 4:* Teams exist to accomplish a mission. Unless a team clearly understands and supports its mission, it will waste resources on nonessential activities.

The makeup of a team (that is, the cast of characters) affects how team members view the ten challenges and fifty best practices introduced in Workpaper #1. Each team member has an opinion about what makes a team effective, and whether or not teams can solve business problems. For example, a dominator already "knows" the result the team should achieve; thus, he or she may choose to disregard best team practices as these may stand in the way of complete control over team activities.

When analyzing the results of the focal team's self-assessment, determine which "characters" are on the team, what type of team it is, and whether the "characters" influence the team negatively. Your assessment will help guide you to select the best-qualified team members and team leadership for the future.

2

The Top-Ten Challenges to Effective Teamwork

Many people believe that the most important factor contributing to success is luck. If you are in the right place, at the right time, and have the right idea, you will succeed. If you are in the wrong place with the right idea at the wrong time, you most probably will fail.

Arguably, luck *is* a factor of success. However, while some luck is due to the chance occurrence of events, other luck happens because people are prepared to be lucky. We can call this second category of luck "self-initiated luck." One example of this occurred when researchers gave everyone in a large group a copy of the day's newspaper and the assignment to count the number of pictures in the newspaper.

Some people in the group performed the task within a few seconds, and reported that there were 43 pictures in the newspaper. The rest of the group took many minutes to go through the newspaper, also finding 43 pictures.

How could one part of the group conclude in only a few seconds that there were 43 pictures, while the rest of the people took so much longer to reach the same conclusion? The answer is that one group of people had self-initiated luck—they read (and trusted) the caption that the researchers had printed under the first picture, which instructed: "Stop counting; there are 43 pictures in the newspaper." This "lucky" group was more observant—and trusting—than the "unlucky" group.[1]

---

[1]Comic-strip creator and illustrator Scott Adams, whom I heard speak some years ago at a conference, shared this "self-initiated luck" anecdote with his audience. Who knows? It may even have been the inspiration for one of Adams' *Dilbert* comic strips!

What can we learn from this example? The primary lesson pertains to the power of observation and how we each can develop and use it—the example shows that as people enlarge their field of perception in their effort to see more things, they, in fact, do see more things. While you presumably have already surmised that this book is not really about luck, self-initiated or otherwise, in teamwork, the point I want to convey is that widening and enlarging your field of perception will help you to better understand why teams are successful or unsuccessful.

This chapter identifies the top-ten challenges that teams must overcome to be successful, addressing the following:

- nine "laws" that inhibit teams from being successful—and how to break them
- the top-ten challenges and how they were identified
- a model for using the information in this book to make teams more successful

"Laws" That Inhibit Team Success

Many teams operate according to team "laws" that inhibit success, preventing their organization from accomplishing its mission. Listed below are some of the laws teams need to break in order to be more successful, followed by lessons I've derived from these laws:

- *If it ain't broke, don't fix it.*[2]
  Lesson: Just because some practice works in some fashion does not mean that it should be left in place without being scrutinized and reevaluated on a regular basis. What is great today may only be good tomorrow and poor the day after. Without constant change, an organization loses its competitive edge.

---

[2]Gerald M. Weinberg, author of numerous wise books that are chock-full of laws such as the ones listed here, is a master at spotting such fallacies. For more on Weinberg's laws and rules, see *The Secrets of Consulting* (New York: Dorset House Publishing, 1985) and *More Secrets of Consulting* (New York: Dorset House Publishing, 2002).

- *We tried it and it doesn't work.*
  Lesson: In many cases, the problem is not what approach a team tried, the problem is the way it implements the solution. Rethinking the way an idea is presented or how a solution is implemented can render previously unsuccessful approaches successful.

- *If you give a child a hammer, everything looks like a nail.*
  Lesson: Many organizations become infatuated with a single idea or technique. For example, if your CEO has bought into the six-sigma approach, the solution to every problem will be to use six-sigma.[3] Unfortunately, what works in one case does not work for every situation.

- *If you keep digging, you'll find a solution.*
  Lesson: When you're in a hole, stop "digging," because if something looks hopeless, it probably is hopeless. Teams must recognize when an idea or approach doesn't work and try something else.

- *Keep the current "thing" alive by using fixes.*
  Lesson: Spending money to keep a system or an automobile or what-have-you running may be the equivalent of throwing money down a rat hole. Many people think that because they already spent X dollars, it is cheaper to spend a few more dollars to keep the old clunker going than to toss it and buy a new system or auto or widget. Recognize when it's better to start over.

- *Rely on the left side of the brain (logic) to solve problems.*
  Lesson: Left-brain thinking limits creativity and innovation, which are right-brain activities. In business, most people rely on left-brain decision-making, impeding both creative thinking and thinking outside of the box. When the CEO of a leading greeting-card company asked a class of kindergartners to raise their hand if they were

---

[3]Motorola originated the concept of six-sigma. The objective is to express the status of a result—the likelihood of defects—in statistical terms. The statement that something is 99.99-percent defect-free (3.4 defects per million) might not sound bad until you think of it in terms of, say, airplane landings.

artists, every child raised a hand. When he asked a group of sixth-graders the same question, very few hands went up. Even fewer hands would be raised if the same question were posed to a group of process-oriented businesspeople. Change this thinking to foster innovation.

- *Always empty the dump truck.*
  Lesson: When developing a proposal, most team members regurgitate everything they know, good and bad, about a project. Developing a "selling" approach within an honest proposal helps focus team members and their project supervisors for success. Sometimes, providing too much information can "un-sell" a project— even for a willing supervisor. Focus on relevant data.

- *If you know the solution, do not share it.*
  Lesson: Often, people know what to do to solve a problem and how to do it, but they don't share this information because they lack the incentive of proper recognition. They are willing to let a specific task fail rather than get involved in solving a problem for which they'll receive neither credit nor compensation. Reward problem-solvers.

- *Never volunteer.*
  Lesson: Many team members feel they have enough work to do without volunteering additional time and resources. Some are even reluctant to volunteer information or to suggest solutions for fear of retaining responsibility for their conjectures. Encourage wise volunteers.

How the Top–Ten Challenges Were Identified

In Chapter 1, I noted that I interviewed hundreds of people for their views on why teams are successful or unsuccessful. After conducting dozens of interviews, I could see a clear pattern in how successful teams handle certain challenges, and so I kept count of the number of times interviewees identified each of these challenges. As part of the collection process, I also identified what I call "best team practices," cited in association with each successful handling of a challenge. From those interviews, I extracted the top-ten challenges (first seen in Workpaper #1 and listed below, the challenges are explored fully in the following ten chapters of this book).

- Challenge 1: Selecting a team leader who will lead
- Challenge 2: Defining team entrance and exit criteria
- Challenge 3: Selecting team members to fulfill specific roles
- Challenge 4: Building trust among team members
- Challenge 5: Training team members to accomplish their assignments
- Challenge 6: Listening to the voice of the customer
- Challenge 7: Breaking down silos
- Challenge 8: Avoiding groupthink
- Challenge 9: Assuring that team efforts are successful
- Challenge 10: Rewarding individual team members

Interrelationships Between Challenges

While organizing survey responses, I took note of the relationships between challenges, eventually concluding that interrelationships can have a greater impact on success or failure than the numerical position of where the challenge comes in the top ten. For example, one challenge may be identified as having been responsible for driving team success, but team members may not have listed that challenge as their biggest.

To better understand what I mean by the importance of inter-relationships between challenges, see Figure 2.1, which organizes the ten challenges for the category called "world-class teamwork." The model begins with *leadership,* which is listed as the first team challenge. Another five of the challenges relate to teamwork done in *preparation* for fulfilling the organization's mission, including defining entrance and exit criteria and selecting and training team members, who must be skilled and motivated as well as fully supported by their organization. Three challenges relate to the *execution* of team tasks, and the final challenge relates to *results,* viewed in terms of team member rewards.

LEADERSHIP → PREPARATION → EXECUTION → RESULTS

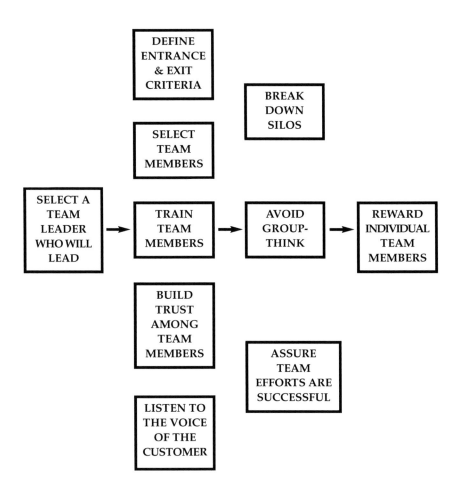

Figure 2.1: Model for World-Class Teamwork.

3

Challenge 1: Selecting a Team Leader Who Will Lead

The title of the person in charge of a team can signal whether that team is, in effect, leaderless. Titles such as "chairperson" and "facilitator," for example, promote the concept that a team can perform effectively regardless of whether or not it has a true leader. I've observed that teams headed by facilitators or chairs recognize that the person nominally in charge of them is not their supervisor and thus lacks supervisory responsibility for individual team members. However, lack of a proper title will not prevent a true leader within a team from leading.

If a team functions as a democracy, it is almost doomed to fail. Democracies are excellent institutions for protecting individuals' rights but they are not necessarily efficient. Many teams function like a ship without a rudder: They may know where they're trying to go but, without a rudder, cannot get there.

Professional sports teams with a winning record are not democracies. A coach selects team members, assigns each player a role, coaches individual players, and determines players' individual objectives. When a football team goes into a huddle, a coach tells players what play to run. It is a time for action; it is not a time to discuss alternatives. If business teams are to function as effectively as sports teams, they need a strong leader, someone who can make decisions, assign specific tasks to team members, and accept responsibility for the success of the team.

Putting the "I" into Selecting a Team Leader Who Will Lead

The "I" in this challenge is the team leader, and is usually the most important "I" on the team. Team leaders have four primary responsibilities. First, they must clearly define the team mission. Their second responsibility is to assemble team members to accomplish the team mission. Third, it is their responsibility to convey the team mission to team members. Fourth, they must motivate team members to accomplish assigned tasks.

A team leader should be the project's manager. He or she does not need to have supervisory authority. However, individual team members' performance appraisals should reflect their effectiveness in fulfilling team tasks. Projects, like teams, should not be run as democracies.

Typical Approach to Selecting a Team Leader

Few organizations bother to write a formal job description for a team leader. Without such a description, most team leaders believe they are responsible for determining when and where their team meets, for preparing a team agenda, and for facilitating discussion. They do not necessarily feel responsible for the success of their team. This lack of ownership can be fatal.

Some organizations select team leaders based solely on seniority. Others appoint whoever declares a team approach as the best way to resolve a business challenge. Occasionally, teams select their own leaders. Some organizations employ facilitators from their training or human resources department, generally individuals with no responsibility for and perhaps minimal knowledge of the team's goals and related work.

Unfortunately, many people view a team leader as someone who determines which way the mob is going, then runs up front and attempts to "lead" it. However, team leaders who attempt to distance themselves from the decision-making process are functioning merely as facilitators, not as leaders. Think back over your experience with team events in business, sports, or not-for-profit groups. My best memories of effective teamwork correlate with teams with strong leaders.

World–Class Approach to Selecting a Team Leader

Tom Landry, one of the great coaches of the National Football League, invariably stood expressionless on the sidelines during even the most intense Dallas Cowboys' football games. I had the opportunity to ask Tom why he never slapped his clipboard or yelled out plays during games, as do so many other NFL coaches. He told me that it was his job to select team members and specialty coaches, train them, develop game plans, and determine who would participate in each game—all in advance of kickoff.

Having assumed responsibility in advance for the team's performance, Landry believed that if he became emotional on the sidelines if a play failed or if the Cowboys were losing, his team members would feel he had lost confidence in the game plan and thus would not be motivated to continue following that plan. Landry was a world-class coach whose approach to teamwork reflected the best practices of an experienced, dedicated, and motivated team leader.

Five Selecting–a–Team–Leader Best Team Practices

I define the qualities we want in a team leader as statements of five best team practices.

- *Leadership Process Best Team Practice 1: Select as team leader an individual who has proven experience as a successful team leader.*

Most successful coaches—in professional sports and elsewhere—learned how to coach by serving under successful, winning coaches. It is no different in business: Individuals selected to lead teams should have previously demonstrated their ability by successfully *helping* to lead a team. Many people believe that leaders are born, not made; I do not. Effective leaders come in all sizes, types, and personalities and they may or may not be naturally charismatic, but what they have in common is that they were all trained by effective leaders.

What differentiates effective leaders from ineffective leaders is their past record of successes. Team owners rarely hire coaches with losing records. Winning coaches attract exciting offers, and are highly sought-after. In sports, it is easy to identify coaches who are successful versus those who are not by looking at the scoreboard. So too in business: Organizations can and should keep a kind of scoreboard to track the success of their team leaders. If an organization does not know whether a team is successful, it cannot judge whether the leader of that team is successful. With various skill levels typically found on any given team, team leaders must be prepared to provide training in order to succeed. Blaming team failure on inferior performers will not cut the mustard. Having a team scoreboard makes it easy to identify who can be successful and who cannot.

- *Leadership Process Best Team Practice 2: Make the team leader responsible for team success.*

Owners and managers of professional sports teams fire coaches when their teams lose, but they usually keep the players. In business, if a project fails, the team members are fired or are given inferior performance ratings, but little accountability is required of the team leader.

To see how this plays out in the world of IT, let's look at a typical, albeit hypothetical, department in a large company. Beginning at the beginning, the parent company decides what physical plant will house the IT group. The IT organization decides what type of computer equipment it will need, what methodologies and other processes it will use to develop software, what individuals to hire to build the software, and what type of training hires will receive. The IT organization also sets the budget and schedule for software development. Given its strong hand in creating the structure, the IT organization should be accountable for the success or failure of the project. Typically, however, if the software development project fails, the project team is blamed for failing and IT management accepts no responsibility for its role in creating the team, the processes, and the environment in which the software was developed.

Responsibility for the success of the team significantly changes the team leader's role and attitude. If I am the team leader but know I will not be responsible, I may lose my motivation for assuring that the team be successful. On the other hand, if I am to be responsible for the success of the team, I know both that my job is on the line and that I will have to put enough additional effort into the team-leadership job to make sure the project is successful.

- *Leadership Process Best Team Practice 3: Empower the team leader to make decisions.*

For years, I taught a course through the Quality Assurance Institute on how to conduct software development reviews. My course had as a prerequisite courses the Institute offered on software development and testing. In the prerequisite courses, students formed into small teams to develop applications software. When the students progressed far enough in my course to perform reviews, they met with their former teammates to review work done by another team. The reviews were structured as helpful, content-centered evaluations, never as criticism of the developers.

Frequently, students asked me by whose authority an IT organization could hold a software development review. Invariably, I answered with a reference to the Bible: Proverbs 11:14 states that in the abundance of counselors there will be victory. Although some translations of this verse use the word "safety" in place of "victory," the message remains the same: All effective leaders solicit advice from counselors, mentors, and advisors to help them make decisions for which they alone will take ultimate responsibility.

All team members provide input, but the important concept for team effectiveness is that the leader makes the decisions. Counselors, mentors, and advisors can effectively aid decision-making so long as they provide advice but do not make decisions. Making decisions involves accepting risk, and while others may mitigate risk, team leaders alone must shoulder responsibility for its acceptance.

- *Leadership Process Best Team Practice 4: Establish the team leader as coach (or mentor) for team members.*

During my career, I have asked many people to perform tasks for me. Many times, the people I ask do not accomplish the task. They offer excuses, claiming they were too busy, or they forgot the due date, or their dog ate their work, and so forth. Eventually, I realized that the primary reason so many individuals do not complete assigned tasks is that they don't know how to do them. They don't ask for help because they don't want to appear incompetent. Once I realized this universal truth, I understood another very important concept in teamwork: Never assume that someone knows how to do the assigned task.

Coaches of sports teams hold tryouts to fill team positions and explain in detail how players need to perform their positions. Coaches put players through practice sessions. Coaches watch them perform. Coaches identify weaknesses in their performance and mold them to do their assigned tasks correctly. Coaches train individuals to be successful.

When a team leader assigns a team member a specific task, the leader is responsible for confirming that the team member can perform that task. Asking whether an individual knows how to perform a given task is not enough; a team leader needs to know where and how the individual performed that task previously. The team leader needs to know how the individual trained, and he or she needs to know the steps that the individual will take to perform that task. If an individual is not fully competent in performing the task, then the team leader needs either to work side-by-side with that individual to assure the task is performed correctly or to choose another team member to work with the individual to demonstrate how to perform the task correctly.

An extremely important role of team leadership is training team members so they are fully competent in performing their assigned tasks.

- *Leadership Process Best Team Practice 5: Make the team leader responsible for motivating team members to accomplish their mission.*

The best way to motivate team members to accomplish tasks and reach team goals is difficult to pinpoint and may change according to personal preferences. Nevertheless, motivation is essential if a team is to be effective. Team leaders can identify ways to motivate people by considering answers to the following questions:

- Why would this person want to be a member of this team?
- Why would this person want to do a task that will not be included in his or her performance appraisal?
- Why would this person want to perform a task for which he or she will not earn reward?

- Why would this person risk not completing regular work in order to perform additional teamwork tasks?

There probably is no single, best way to motivate teams or individuals. Some people are motivated by money or recognition; some relish challenging tasks; some do not want to let down other team members who are depending on them to complete a task.

Successful team leaders learn how to motivate individuals. They develop a process that generally begins by ensuring that each team member clearly understands the team mission, how success will be determined, each individual's role, how each member will be rewarded based on fulfilling assigned roles, and how each member will contribute to team success. The team leader must be sure that each team member buys into accomplishing tasks and recognizes the importance of the team mission to the success of the organization.

Motivation must be reinforced and replenished every day. It is to be expected that at one point or another, people will experience highs and lows in their work life, as well as personal problems in their home life, but effective team leaders will take all of these into account and continually encourage and support each team member to fulfill his or her responsibilities.

Impediments to the Team–Leader Challenge

Organizations face numerous conflicts between their tendency to appoint strong team leaders and their desire to create fully functioning teams. For example, conflict often arises in connection with management's fear that elevating one person to the position of team leader will downplay the role of individuals on the team—as a result, many organizations encourage team members to work together in developing a consensus approach in order to accomplish the team mission. For such organizations, having a strong team leader frequently is seen as threatening to the ability of the team to function as a cohesive unit.

A second impediment standing in the way of a strong team leader's drive to lead is that team members generally do not regard the leader as their bona fide supervisor. It is a problem that, in most organizations, individuals on a team are evaluated on how well or poorly they perform their own part of the job, not on how well they perform as *members of a team*. If the team leader has no real say in performance reviews and how individuals are evaluated, it is difficult for him or her to function in the leadership role.

A third major impediment to finding strong team leaders is that, in many organizations, the person who speaks with the most authority or who takes charge of matters before others step forward may appear to be the obvious leader but is not necessarily the best choice. Selecting the most senior person, for example, may be the wrong choice.

Strategies to Overcome the Team–Leader Challenge

Three strategies that can help overcome impediments to developing strong team leaders follow:

1. Adopt the sports team model.

The best team model is the professional sports team on which both teamwork and leadership are needed. In sports, the coach is the leader—if he or she is effective and has the respect of all team members, they will be motivated to fulfill their roles to win the game.

2. Involve team leaders in team members' performance appraisals.

Effective employees do what is necessary for their organization to succeed. Send the message that teamwork is an important part of everyone's job by rating it the same way other work is rated.

3. Select a team leader who can work well with team members.

A leader's people skills are often more valuable and mission-critical than his or her technical skills. Choose with this criterion in mind.

Team–Leader Plan of Action

If organizations want strong team leaders, management must support their cultivation. An effective approach is to write a team-leader job description. The job description should incorporate the concepts included in the five leadership best team practices detailed in this chapter.

Management should evaluate team leadership as a stepping-stone to promotion, and offer opportunities for individuals to demonstrate leadership capabilities. These team-leadership skills are the same skills needed by individuals if they are to move to a higher level in the organization. Management needs to evaluate the effectiveness of the individuals appointed as team leaders, and use that assessment to help identify candidates for promotion.

4

Challenge 2:
Defining Team Entrance
and Exit Criteria

It has been said that if you don't know where you are going, all roads lead there. Many teams operate as if they do not *want* a defined destination. "All roads lead there" is a perfect scapegoat: When a team finishes a project, it can declare victory no matter what, because there is no way to determine whether or not it met its objective.

Entrance criteria define basic circumstances that must exist before a team can begin work, as well as all information the team will need at the start. Exit criteria define the attributes of the deliverables that the team must produce. For example, if you were going to bake a cake, entrance criteria could include a recipe, ingredients, measuring cups and bowls, spoons and other utensils, an oven, and a cook. Exit criteria could include the desired consistency of the cake; its flavor, height, and diameter; the number of layers; and, perhaps, the type and thickness of the icing. Exit criteria also could include a description, drawing, or photograph of the finished cake.

Professional sports teams carefully define entrance and exit criteria for their training camps. For example, entrance criteria for team members might state that players must have a specified level of physical fitness and demonstrate some level of ability in the sport. Exit criteria for someone finishing training camp may include being able to run one-hundred yards in ten seconds, to bench-press three-hundred pounds, and to understand the attributes of the position assigned. Players who do not meet the entrance criteria are not invited to training camp and players who cannot achieve the training-camp exit criteria do not make the team.

It is much easier for a business organization's management to create a loosely organized team than it is to define team entrance and exit criteria. When managers define entrance and exit criteria, they accept responsibility for team success; if entrance and exit criteria go undefined, management can blame the team itself if the team fails to achieve the goals management foists upon it.

Putting the "I" into Defining Team Entrance and Exit Criteria

Defining entrance and exit criteria for a team as an entity is as important as defining criteria for each team member. When coaching the Dallas Cowboys, Tom Landry accepted responsibility for the team, whether it won or lost. None of the players was responsible for winning, but each player was responsible for meeting objectives defined for him by Tom Landry. If a player met the objectives—the exit criteria—established by Landry, he earned reward regardless of whether the team won or lost.

Putting the "I" back into teams—in this case, in terms of entrance and exit criteria—means that each team member must meet specific entrance and exit criteria. Executing Landry's approach may or may not have led the team to win. Many teams I have been a part of have had a few "workers" and many "hangers-on." The hangers-on made only minor contributions to the team effort, but they received the same reward as the workers if the team succeeded. Hangers-on can move up their organization's career ladder by attaching themselves to teams that include the organization's top performers.

This is not only unfair, it is also bad for business. Team members who make the greatest contributions should receive the greatest rewards, and those who barely contribute should receive no reward (except perhaps a pink slip). Putting the "I" back into teams means defining, as concretely and objectively as possible, entrance and exit criteria for a team and for each team member. Team members should not begin working until they meet entrance criteria, and should not stop working until they achieve exit criteria. Individual team members should be held accountable for meeting their entrance criteria and achieving their exit criteria.

Typical Approach to Defining Entrance and Exit Criteria

Many businesses exhort team members to think outside the box. Since there is no specific definition for this process, people assign their own meaning to the term. To most people, "thinking outside the box" means that there are no constraints that affect their assignment. Individuals are free to roam into new plans and developments whenever they feel the urge.

In this author's opinion, thinking outside the box possibly is one of the greatest wastes of a team's time. The productivity problem with thinking outside the box is that it is an uncontrolled team activity. It may produce some wonderful results, but if those results are not needed to accomplish the work assigned to a team, they are meaningless.

Searching for the word "innovation" on the Internet leads to millions of resources. Searching for the words "managed innovation" or "managing innovation," however, yields significantly fewer hits. To me, this evidences that people confuse *thinking outside the box* with being innovative, free of constraints. Uncontrolled innovation can be interesting but nonproductive while *managing innovation* (by focusing on exit criteria) can be difficult but very productive.

Organizations need to manage innovation by defining entrance and exit criteria for every goal they seek. Thomas Edison, for example, described an exit criterion for one of his endeavors as "a globe that glowed." Edison spent a lot of time brainstorming, thinking outside the box, and pursuing various dead-ends in his effort to reach his goal, eventually producing the electric light bulb. Although Edison clearly must have done a considerable amount of thinking outside the box (an activity I prefer to call "creative thinking"), he always remained focused on his exit criteria, maintaining that the dead-ends were not failures, they just taught him multiple ways *not* to make an electric light bulb.

World–Class Approach to Defining Entrance and Exit Criteria

When my children were young, I told them again and again that they needed to keep their rooms "clean." However, I never defined either the entrance criteria or the exit criteria for "clean." As a result, my children defined their own entrance criteria when their mother or I sent them to their rooms to clean up the mess. Likewise, my children also defined their exit criteria, which to them was a room with no visible mess. They shoved toys and other belongings under the beds, threw clothing into the closets, and stuffed objects into bureau drawers. Without defined exit criteria for a clean room, they felt free to shove, throw, and stuff clothes and possessions out of sight rather than hang, fold, or stack things neatly.

If I had been a world-class parent, I would have defined entrance and exit criteria for the assignment of a clean room. The entrance criteria might have been that my children would begin cleaning their rooms before they left for school in the morning. If I had provided them with exit criteria—such as, (1) all clothes must be hung up in the closets or neatly folded in bureau drawers; (2) all toys must be placed on shelves in the closets or on the bookcases; (3) the beds must be made neatly, with sheets and blankets tucked in; and (4) no trash on the floors—we all would have understood the goal of the assignment. My children could have innovated how to clean their rooms, but not been free to innovate the exit criteria of a clean room.

Both the process for defining entrance and exit criteria and the process for motivating and guiding a team to work toward achieving exit criteria are treated extensively in the remaining sections of this chapter. Material in the preceding chapter as well as sections in the eight chapters that follow this chapter will help you better define entrance and exit criteria as seen in the context of the other challenges. For example, Chapter 3 shines a light on leadership as an entrance criterion, making clear the point that a team should not begin work until *a team leader who will lead* is found and assigned to propel the team to meet objectives.

Five Defining–Entrance–and–Exit–Criteria Best Team Practices

- *Entrance-and-Exit-Criteria Process Best Team Practice 1: Define entrance criteria before teamwork begins.*

Unless a team defines and achieves entrance criteria *before begin-ning* an assignment, it begins with a handicap it may never over-come. I sometimes illustrate the importance of establishing well-defined entrance criteria in the following way: Several days after work on a project lacking well-defined entrance criteria has begun, I invite the team to join me for a sociable coffee break. I offer to bake the team's favorite cookies for the event. However, unbe-knownst to the team, I corrupt the recipe by omitting one delicious ingredient and substituting a nasty-tasting ingredient in its place. When baked, the cookies taste awful.

Team members arrive for the break, eager to bite into the cookies. Expecting a delicious treat, they immediately know some-thing is wrong. When asked why the cookies taste terrible, I point out that all the ingredients for the cookies—the entrance criteria—were not fully defined. Team members rapidly see the analogy: When entrance criteria are not properly and fully specified, the failure can prevent the team from achieving its objective.

To succeed, a team should have as entrance criteria most or all of the following elements:

- team members who are qualified to fulfill their roles
- a team leader who will lead
- a team meeting-agenda template
- a recorder who will record and publish meeting minutes
- space in which to meet
- adequate time and resources to complete team objectives
- management support for exit criteria
- authority to do the tasks needed to complete the team's assignment
- background materials on the assignment
- current performance statistics related to the assignment

With these elements secured, management must make the team leader fully cognizant that he or she is responsible for seeing that the team meets all entrance criteria before team activities begin.

As surely is clear from the preceding discussion, teams all too frequently are tempted to start work before meeting all entrance criteria—behavior that gives rise to the view that there is never enough money to do X right the first time, but there's always enough to correct the mistakes. The message: Plan and organize resources for success the first time around.

- *Entrance-and-Exit-Criteria Process Best Team Practice 2: Define exit criteria in measurable terms before team activities begin.*

Imagine that you embark on a diet to lose weight, but you do not know how much you weighed before you started to diet and you do not weigh yourself when you finish dieting. Without any measurable entrance or exit criteria, you can declare the diet a success whenever you want. The same unfortunately is true for many teams—without measurable criteria, they can declare success.

During my years as a software project manager, I always visualized and documented a plan for three different software deliverables (exit criteria) for any given development project. For example, as the first deliverable, I would identify *a version that could exceed customer expectations.* I would accomplish this by continually reworking requirements until I was sure they met the true needs of my customer.

My second visualized version of the software deliverable was *a version that would meet the documented requirements* (projecting the case in which the deliverable would satisfy the contract whether or not it would satisfy the customer). The primary benefit of this version was that the methods I used to develop the software would be defendable in court.

My third visualization of the deliverable was *a version I could complete on time and within budget.* To plan this, I carefully identified attributes of the software that would not have to be complete prior to releasing the software into operation. Such attributes, the inclusion of which could be postponed or possibly eliminated entirely, could include detail-level documentation, testing beyond a basic level, training of users, and compliance with IT standards that I knew were destined to be replaced. This method could result in excessive software maintenance, but the cost and time associated with that maintenance was incorporated in another budget and schedule, and thus was not my responsibility. The benefit of this version was that, merely for meeting the original schedule and budget, I earned reward as an outstanding software project leader even though I behaved regrettably.

These three visualizations of each deliverable gave me what I came to regard as "wiggle room." The more wiggle room incorporated into exit criteria, the more leeway a team has. To see exactly what I mean by wiggle room, let's suppose you are building a home and specify one exit criterion as "painted walls." Painters assigned that exit criterion will decide what you failed to specify: They will decide whether to paint the walls in the house but not in the garage or basement. They will decide whether to apply a primer. They will decide whether one coat of paint is enough even though it may not cover seams in the wallboards. They will decide whether they can use any brand of paint.

- *Entrance-and-Exit-Criteria Process Best Team Practice 3: Define the procedures that the team will use in order to meet exit criteria.*

Entrance and exit criteria identify what a team needs to do. They do not define how to do it. Consider a basketball player shooting free throws. The entrance criterion is a referee's call of a foul on the opposing team's player. Exit criteria, one of which may be that a specific basketball player should make 60 percent of his or her free throws, are established by the coach and are reinforced by practice drills. To establish 60-percent accuracy as a reachable exit criterion, the coach first must train the player to sink six out of ten free throws.

Team members also need to be trained—but their training is knowledge-based rather than physical, and is geared to show them how their team operates and how they will fulfill their role as members of a specific team. For example, individual team members should know team protocol: No meeting will be held without an agenda, no meeting will last longer than one hour, no meeting will be held unless all team members are present, and so forth, all of which depend on the very important aspect of an organization's having developed detailed team procedures.

To gauge the importance of training, let's switch gears from the basketball scenario given above to football and teams in the NFL: Each team plays sixteen football games during the regular season. Each game has one hour of playing time, plus timeouts and penalties, both of which considerably extend the "real" time from kickoff until the end of the fourth quarter. The maximum amount of playing time a team member may have during a regular season cannot exceed sixteen hours, but that same team member may practice a thousand hours or more each season preparing for those sixteen hours of official game play. Training is the secret, a secret that pertains to IT people attempting to build an effective team as well as to players on the sports field. Team members and management—whether in IT or in sports—must be committed to the idea that a team cannot function effectively without proper, extensive training.

- *Entrance-and-Exit-Criteria Process Best Team Practice 4: Assign a judge to monitor discussion and team activities in the context of exit criteria.*

In my foray into playful stereotyping in Chapter 1's discussion of the cast of characters that materialize at team meetings, I noted characters such as the Talker, the Dominator, the Detailer, the Destroyer, the Intimidator, and the Judge, among others. The point to note here is that even though a team may have well-defined entrance and exit criteria, team members may tend to revert to their stereotypical roles. For example, the Talker may offer dissertations on selected topics that bore most of the team members and are not focused on the exit criteria. The Detailer may continually discuss the lowest level of detail even though some of the decisions affecting that detail should not yet be made. The Destroyer may try to cut off discussion too soon so that potential alternatives languish. The Intimidator may imply that, for various reasons, only one approach is acceptable. The Dominator may try to take over the role of the team leader.

The Judge may be the team leader or another well-respected member of the team. The role of the Judge is to rule when team activities are not productive. For example, if the Detailer gets into too low a level of detail, the Judge can cut off that discussion and refocus attention on issues that need to be addressed first.

The concept of appointing someone to act as judge is as important as are his or her actions. A judge should stop unproductive discussion and activities. Understanding the function of a judge should affect how teams operate.

While applying this concept may seem unfair or threaten to cut off productive discussion, it works. In an earlier chapter, I noted that teams should not operate as democracies. There is no true democracy in an organization. An organization has a charter, a specific mission, vision, and values. Organizations charge employees to operate within those ground rules. For example, if an organization assigns its IT department to build software for its internal business units, the IT department cannot decide to begin building software to sell commercially. The role of a judge is to assure that the activities undertaken by a team stay focused on meeting exit criteria in the most effective and efficient manner.

- *Entrance-and-Exit-Criteria Process Best Team Practice 5: Prepare team members to meet the team's exit criteria.*

Most young kids would not try out for a Pop Warner football team without having practiced throwing a football, kicking a football, and running passes along the length of a field. Before trying out, young players should have learned some of the basic rules and techniques of the game. Similarly, businesspeople assigned to a team also should prepare to fulfill their position by learning team skills. Some people prepare by watching how experienced professionals perform on teams. Others ask senior members for guidance when faced with a new task.

Many college quarterbacks who are talented enough to be drafted by an NFL team sit on the bench during games for the first year or more of their career. It is during this bench-sitting time that, by watching how the pros play the quarterback position, new drafts prepare themselves mentally and physically to eventually be the Number 1 quarterback for an NFL team. Of course, all their hours of practice, workouts, and watching game videos work in combination with the locker-room pep talks and on-the-field training they receive from skilled coaches and managers, and may have just a little bit to do with their chances of success, injuries not withstanding.

Most IT employees will be assigned to many different teams during their career. The organizations they work for will be wise to motivate employees to undergo a lot of potentially unrewarding and unspectacular preparation, which, like bench-sitting, should be designed to train them to become spectacular team members who produce spectacular results.

Some of the knowledge and skills individuals should possess prior to being assigned to a team include the following:

- conflict resolution methods
- knowledge of the organization's standards and procedures for team activities
- use of team tools and techniques (such as brainstorming)
- methods on how to "sell" ideas (such as are discussed in books by persuasion professionals)
- ability to recognize workable versus untenable strategies and ideas

Former NFL star quarterback Roger Staubach commented, "Perseverance and resiliency are the number-one qualities of a competitor."[1] These qualities are essential for business-team members as well as for members of sports teams. Staubach also noted that everyone gets knocked down periodically—quite literally in football while usually only figuratively in other walks of life. With proper preparation and despite setbacks, team members need to be able to pick themselves up to continue pursuing project goals. They must be ready to maintain team values and to carry out their leader's plan.

Impediments to the Defining-Entrance-and-Exit-Criteria Challenge

Three major impediments that business teams face in defining entrance and exit criteria for assignments are discussed in the paragraphs that follow.

The first obstacle occurs when *senior management overly controls accountability* by defining entrance and exit criteria and by determining resources and other materials to be allocated to the team. The team leader needs to be heavily involved in defining entrance criteria—which in effect define the makeup of the team, and the resources and materials allocated to it—and exit criteria if they are to be able to take credit for their team's success (or be held accountable for its failure).

By selecting his players, determining how they would train, and defining their exit criteria, Tom Landry made it explicit that

---

[1] "How I Compete," Roger Staubach, *BusinessWeek,* August 21-28, 2006, p. 59.

the outcome of every Dallas Cowboys' game, whether won or lost, was his responsibility and his alone. However, as I have noted above, once in the game, individual team members were accountable for playing the assigned position according to how each had been thoroughly trained and coached. Unfortunately, many IT managers who themselves determine parameters and resources seem to prefer to hold their workers accountable for failure but give themselves credit for success.

The second problem teams face is that they mistakenly believe that *doing the job of defining entrance and exit criteria properly takes "too long,"* believing as well that the team could be put together and start work much more quickly if entrance and exit criteria did not have to be defined. For decades, software developers have wanted to begin to write code long before project requirements and design are finalized. They are right in maintaining that coding can *begin* more quickly without the wait for completion of fully specified requirements and design, but the results can be disastrous or useless.

Believing defined entrance and exit criteria limit a team's ability to "think outside the box" constitutes the third major obstacle a team faces. Entrance and exit criteria can limit activities in which a team might otherwise engage, but the limitation argument has as much merit as does the argument debating whether obeying traffic lights increases or decreases an individual's rights. Perhaps following traffic laws decreases the rights of individuals to move about as they may wish, but obeying traffic laws and lights, at the very least, facilitates the movement of traffic. Similarly, one purpose of entrance and exit criteria is to define a team and its objectives. Another is to facilitate effective, efficient movement of work toward successful project completion.

Strategies to Overcome the Defining–Entrance–and–Exit–Criteria Challenge

Three strategies that teams can use to overcome impediments to defining entrance and exit criteria before beginning teamwork are discussed below.

1. Make management (including the team leader) accountable for the results produced by its employees.

If management hires workers, provides them with necessary training to do their job, establishes work processes, assigns work, and monitors progress, then management cannot transfer full accountability for success or failure to workers. Follow the professional sports model: A player's responsibility is to play his or her position as flawlessly as possible. If the team loses, fire the coach.

2. Develop a winning process and follow it.

If experience shows that defining entrance and exit criteria increases a team's effectiveness and efficiency, spend the time it takes to adequately define those criteria. To see the truth in this principle, think about how most adults assemble parts to form a finished product—for example, a child's toy. Many of us think we can accomplish the task more quickly by opening the box and putting parts together rather than first spending time reading the directions and then assembling the toy, adhering to the premise, "If all else fails, read the directions." If you think it takes too long to define entrance and exit criteria in relationship to the total resources needed to complete an assignment, you're barking up the wrong tree.

3. Restrict thinking outside the box to entrance and exit criteria constraints.

Following a strategy of defining and satisfying entrance and exit criteria does not inhibit innovation and creativity; rather, it focuses innovation. An example of this is the well-known cereal manufacturer that established an exit criterion requiring that cereal not become soggy for at least three minutes after the addition of milk or another liquid. This goal focused the development team's effort and prevented it from performing any work that would not contribute to the defined criterion.

Entrance-and-Exit-Criteria Plan of Action

The plan of action for defining and using entrance and exit criteria for team assignments calls for transferring, directly or indirectly, much of the accountability for success to management. Therefore, unless management supports the time required to define entrance and exit criteria, and then enforces those criteria, the process will not work.

To assure that people are defining entrance and exit criteria correctly and thoroughly, have them follow two steps:

- Step 1: Develop entrance and exit criteria standards.
- Step 2: Enforce entrance and exit criteria.

It is not enough just to require definition of entrance and exit criteria. *Develop specific standards* to guide both management and team members on what should be included in entrance and exit criteria. From this chapter and the chapters that detail the other nine challenges, readers can derive the fullest definition of entrance and exit criteria.

The process of developing standards and writing procedures incorporating entrance and exit criteria is meaningless unless management will *enforce strict adherence to defined criteria.* Unless the team leader concurs that entrance criteria are met, team activities should not commence. Likewise, team activities should continue only when deliverables are confirmed. Exception to this procedure can arise only if management decides to override the exit criteria.

5

Challenge 3:
Selecting Team Members
for Specific Roles

Former Notre Dame football coach Lou Holtz employed an especially effective technique to illustrate to his team the importance of each player's fulfilling his assigned role. If, for example, a lineman assigned to protect the quarterback didn't exert himself at practice—perhaps because he considered himself, as one of eleven defensive players, to be only a minor part of the team—Coach Holtz removed that player from the line without replacing him, leaving a defensive line that was missing one player to try to protect the quarterback. When Coach Holtz resumed the practice session, the quarterback invariably would get immediately sacked, and would get sacked on each subsequent play. Coach Holtz's lesson was clear: The team could not succeed unless every player performed his assigned role to the highest standard—as if his own and his teammates' lives depended on it.

Coach Holtz presumably felt justified teaching this harsh lesson because he knew he picked the very best eleven players to play defense from the many who competed for positions on Notre Dame's revered football team. Once selected by Coach Holtz, players were expected to give their all to improve their skills during the many practice hours each week. Compare Coach Holtz's approach to player selection to that of your organization's team-member-selection approach. Do you select the best available person to fill each spot? Do people train to master their team responsibilities? Are team members assigned specific roles to perform during team activities?

Putting the "I" into Selecting Team Members

The concept of "one person, one vote" does not lead to successful team performance. Professional sports teams do not vote on what plays they execute. The "one person, one vote" approach also works poorly in business. An effective team has only one vote: the team leader's vote. Most successful leaders listen to team members but make decisions alone. The most important decisions a team leader must make are, first, what team-member roles a project requires and, second, how to select people to fulfill those roles.

Imagine that you want to put together a team to build a payroll system. One possible approach would be to select three people and then begin discussions with each of them about how to build the payroll system. A second possible approach would be to select someone knowledgeable about payroll taxes to work on that aspect of the software, another person knowledgeable about company benefits to work on the benefits component of the software, and a third person knowledgeable about how individuals in the organization report task-specific hours-worked to develop the time-reporting component of the software.

Following the first approach, you would select three random people to brainstorm ways to build a payroll system; in the second, you first would define roles needed to build a successful payroll system, then you would identify team members to fulfill those roles. When selecting people for a football team, a coach may choose a person who weighs one-hundred-and-fifty pounds to be a receiver but would want a three-hundred-pound player on the offensive line. In most lines of business, personal attributes such as size and weight rarely matter—or certainly matter less than on the football field—but specific knowledge and skills matter enormously.

In addition to selecting prepared, able team members, a team leader must also identify each team member's potential engagement and compliance with an assigned role. Consider the team-member-selection process from the perspective of an individual selected for the team. Team leaders should know how each team member will answer the following questions:

- Why was I selected to be on the team?
- What is my assignment as a team member?
- How will my performance be evaluated?
- What competencies are needed to fulfill my assigned role?
- Do I need additional skills to fulfill my team assignment?
- Will I be provided with training if I do not have all needed skills?
- What are the roles of the other members of the team?
- How will I interact with other team members?
- Am I an important member of the team?

Typical Approach to Selecting Team Members

After interviewing hundreds of team members to determine what criteria they believe caused their selection for a specific team, I identified many valid reasons why people were selected (discussed later in this chapter in "Five Team-Member-Selection Best Team Practices"), but also a surprisingly high occurrence of common but unprofessional and irrelevant reasons, some of which are listed below:

- The individual was a friend of the team leader.
- The individual graduated from the same college or was in the same fraternity as the rest of the team members.
- The individual was identified by management as being on the beach and therefore was available to participate on the team.
- The individual openly opposed proposed changes and was brought onto the team to help present objections.
- The individual was known for supplying doughnuts and cookies for team meetings.

These seemingly silly but common reasons exist because many organizations fail to develop an effective approach to selecting team members to fulfill specific team assignments. All organizations need to establish detailed procedures on how to staff teams. If no formal process to select team members for specific roles is in place, the team-member-selection process will flounder; even worse, because no formal process exists, it cannot be improved.

If organizations have neither a formal process for selecting members, nor a proscribed process for determining whether or not the team has been successful, it is no wonder that most teams fail. To protect against project failure, the organization must define a procedure for how to staff a team, and also must specify how the selection process can be improved.

World–Class Approach to Selecting Team Members

The formation of a legendary orchestra is an excellent example of a world-class approach to selecting team members to fulfill specific roles. Glenn Miller was one of the most successful bandleaders of the swing era. His recordings are still readily available, and many bands still copy the Glenn Miller approach.

As documented in the film *The Glenn Miller Story,* Miller continually sought the right "sound." Once he found the sound he wanted, he put together a band that would produce that sound. The sound uniquely emphasized certain musical instruments and combinations of ensembles within the band. When his orchestra played a song, everyone knew it was a Glenn Miller rendition. Even today, songs like "In the Mood" are known as Glenn Miller classics.

To discover potential bandleaders capable of conducting musicians to create his unique sound, Miller played a game I call "Bet Your Career" in which he would identify the sound he wanted (the exit criteria) and then would put a "team" in place (in Miller's case, of course, the team was made up of musicians). If nobody liked the new band's sound, Miller knew that the musician was not the right man for the job.

Let's see how we might build a world-class business team according to the Glenn Miller approach. First, we'd find a motivated and hardworking team leader. Next, we'd empower the leader to select each team member to fulfill a specific role to achieve the "sound." Then, we'd let the team members know why they were selected, and what type of sound they must produce. We'd encourage them to exhibit appropriate enthusiasm and a willingness to work to achieve the team's objective. Then, we'd set them loose and assess the result.

The world-class approach to selecting team members to fulfill specific roles is one of the ten team challenges that must be addressed if the team is to be successful. To learn in finer detail about team-member selection, consider the five best team practices discussed in the next section.

Five Team–Member–Selection Best Team Practices

- *Team-Member-Selection Process Best Team Practice 1: Define the composition of the team in terms of meeting exit criteria.*

Team members who are selected for a given team must possess whatever skills will be needed to achieve the team's assignments. No matter whether a team will need to produce a specific sound, build a software project, select a subcontractor, or develop a work plan, people selected for the team should be competent to accomplish the specific task.

To determine a team's composition, the team leader should identify what kinds of jobs will need to be done as well as the number of people who will be needed to perform each job described. For instance, an individual who is selected to perform administrative tasks (such as serving as recording secretary) should possess the necessary skills. Each team member should be selected because he or she possesses the necessary skill or knowledge for the team to be successful, although training may be elected. Exit criteria help define what team skills are needed for a project.

Obviously, specific constraints can affect the team leader's determination of team composition (for example, a limited budget, an unusually tight schedule, or an insufficient pool of individuals available to participate on the team). Taking constraints and limitations into account, leaders must select team members only after they have thoroughly defined team roles.

- *Team-Member-Selection Process Best Team Practice 2: Identify the most suitable individual to fulfill each defined team role.*

Before recruiting members for a team, leaders will want to identify characteristics and skills needed by whoever will perform specific tasks. Ideally, individuals can be identified by name, but it may only be feasible to identify specific skill sets. For example, a leader may believe that the recording secretary needs proficient grammatical and writing skills as well as have the ability to abstract and summarize key points made by others. Leaders should never select all members of a team without first having determined who among them will be capable of serving, say, as recording secretary.

A popular, and cynical, analogy likens teams to a camel—a horse built by committee. This comparison resonates with many teams' experiences: The probability of success is almost zero when a team is ill-conceived and poorly formed, as if put together by a committee of disparate strangers. Cohesive, effective teams rarely form by chance.

Regrettably, many team leaders do not do the necessary homework before selecting team members. They assume that any team will be cohesive, getting all members together to take effective action. Not so: If a leader wants a winning team, he or she should do the research needed to fill specific team roles with the best possible candidates. Selecting role models like Glenn Miller can dramatically increase the team's probability of success.

- *Team-Member-Selection Process Best Team Practice 3: Recruit team members who are qualified to fill the defined team roles.*

After identifying optimal candidates, a leader must take all steps necessary to successfully hire them as team members. Because there is a difference between "selected" or "ordained" team members and "recruited" candidates, leaders must take care to *recruit* rather than merely fill a position with a warm body. By this I mean that unlike "selection," in which you simply inform individuals that they are now members of the team, "recruiting" implies selling an individual on the merits of joining the team, and only accepting the individual as a team member when he or she buys into working to make the team successful. With "selection," one *assumes* that the individual has the proper motivation, time, and attitude to work as an effective team member, but it does not go the extra step to *confirm* that the assumption is correct.

In more than a few organizations, people really don't want to work on a team and, if assigned, do as little work as possible to help make the team, as a whole, successful, preferring to put their greatest effort into tasks that will reflect kindly on themselves as individuals. Assigning such unmotivated individuals to a team, whether they are qualified to perform the work or not, almost always is detrimental to the team.

On the other hand, recruiting people who take pride in being part of a winning team is an effective strategy. Team leaders who can offer candidates a slot on a winning team give them an opportunity with true value. To help sell the candidate on the merits of the team during recruitment, team leaders may be able to allude to ways the candidate will enjoy certain benefits, such as the following:

- "Such potential benefits as X and Z almost certainly will be gained by participating on this team."
- "Your current skill sets—A and C, for example—can be enhanced by membership on this team."
- "Team objectives, something we call 'exit criteria,' will play a prominent role in how you as an individual working on the team will be evaluated."
- "Because you'll only be expected to spend J amount of time on teamwork, you'll be able to use P or more hours to practice your favorite avocation."
- "Our team leaders solicit the support of each individual's supervisor—so you'll have all the time you need for teamwork as part of your normal workday."
- "The role you'll play on the team is an important one and the skills you'll bring will be critical to its success—I'm confident you'll be a crucial member of a winning team."

- *Team-Member-Selection Process Best Team Practice 4: Provide training to enhance existing skills and to supplement missing skills.*

When coaches recruit players for a sports team, they do not expect them to be fully proficient in all needed skills. Part of a coach's job is to prepare drills that, through practice and repetition, will train players to improve. One strategy a sports coach may try is the introduction of new or different methods.

Business teams can be approached in a similar fashion. Once leaders have recruited all members for the business team, they should provide training for individuals either to help them learn new skills or to supplement existing skills. Skills supplementation can include: *coaching*—a practice in which the team leader or a senior member of the team partners with an individual to oversee the successful completion of assignments; *pairing*—a practice in which team members work together to complete assignments; and *importing experts*—a practice in which external consultants add the missing competencies.

Team leaders must recognize the need for team-member training and skills supplementation. This means that team leaders will allocate time and resources to provide necessary training, or that they will secure the time and effort of individuals outside the team to supplement team-member skills.

• *Team-Member-Selection Process Best Team Practice 5: Identify potential back-up members to fill in for team members as needed.*

A football coach knows that a player may not be able to perform an assignment because of injury or an off day. The coach knows that, at some point in time, he may need to replace that player with another. A business-team leader must also consider and plan for people who can serve as back-up or replacement staff in case a team member cannot complete the assignment because of reasons such as illness, incompetence, lack of motivation, transfer, or a conflicting assignment.

Making a best practice of identifying back-up team members or strategies for a contingency plan is neither time-consuming nor difficult. All a team leader need do is list the names of individual team members and the tasks for which each is responsible, annotating the list with his or her plan for replacing individuals if necessary. The plan can be as simple as either indicating that the leader can perform the tasks of the individual who is leaving the team or reassigning the tasks to other team members. The plan might designate a consultant to replace a project-critical member, reduce the number or complexity of deliverables planned for a specific release, or delay completion of exit criteria. Whatever their strategy, project leaders should prioritize team objectives to determine which ones to reduce or eliminate if necessary.

Impediments to the Team–Member–Selection Challenge

Three factors that team leaders must carefully consider when selecting team members solely based on their expected performance relate to supervisory support, candidate motivation, and competence. Be wary when difficulties of the following nature loom during the selection process.

The first potential difficulty arises when *the candidate's supervisor openly opposes his or her participation on the proposed team.* Opposition may result from a supervisor's fear that tasks for which he or she is responsible will not be accomplished if the candidate is diverted to the team. A supervisor's own performance evaluation may be based partly on seeing that specific, assigned tasks are accomplished, a goal that may not be feasible to reach without all hands on board.

A supervisor's reluctance to authorize a subordinate's team participation may intensify if the team assignment is open-ended. A supervisor who depends on a specific individual to complete a high-priority assignment will want to keep the individual working on the assignment rather than authorize work on a team. It is crucial that team leaders clearly articulate every benefit derived from permitting team participation—for both the affected supervisor and the organization as a whole.

A second area to watch pertains to whether *the candidate is or is not genuinely motivated to be part of the team.* There are many reasons someone may not want to participate on a team. For example, some people worry whether performance reviews will be based on their individual performance or on the performance of the team as a body. Others may not want to participate on a team because they flat out do not like team activities, or they do not like the team leader, or they have issues with other members of the team, or, perhaps most distasteful of all, they do not like the team's objective.

A third area to assess is *candidate competence.* Does the candidate express complete confidence about accomplishing tasks? No one wants responsibility for tasks for which his or her probability of success is very low. For example, if a team activity involves using a specific tool or technique, and the individual does not feel competent, he or she most likely will not want to become a member of that team. When a candidate knows team-activity expectations during the selection process, he or she will reveal confidence about performing them—if a candidate lacks confidence, the team leader should look elsewhere, quickly.

Strategies to Overcome the Team–Member–Selection Challenge

Three strategies for selecting stellar team members should be in every leader's tool kit.

1. Illustrate the value of team success to both the supervisor and the organization.

This first strategy derives from the leader's grasp of the value the team will provide to the organization and team members' supervisors. Effective team-member recruiting addresses challenges to the recruitment process. The most effective strategy to overcome a supervisor's resistance to appointing an individual to a team is to demonstrate to that supervisor that he or she will receive recognition for releasing individuals to teamwork, thus providing value to the organization. In such a case, the supervisor will probably be more than willing to approve an individual's team participation.

2. Address a potential team member's concerns as to personal reward.

A second strategy is to answer "What's in it for me" (WIIFM), a common worry. Putting the "I" in team means designing a win-win situation for an individual and a team. People grow tired of working hard only to see reward going to someone else. However, contributing to the success of an organization can be a source of motivation. Team leaders should recruit members by describing benefits to individuals as well as by detailing how the individuals themselves will provide benefit to the organization.

3. Provide a powerful incentive in the form of training.

When screening candidates for team participation, leaders can offer to train people to more successfully participate in team activities, but still demonstrate confidence in each individual's potential. By increasing an individual's competency through training, the leader increases the individual's ability to earn positive performance appraisals and career advancement—all good things. The leader must assure that the estimated schedule and the budget for team activities incorporate adequate resources and time to train individuals to fulfill team responsibilities.

Team–Member–Selection Plan of Action

Building a team with defined member roles is a process. Each team leader in an organization should not have to invent and execute a new team-recruitment method. If the process for team-member selection is predefined, all team leaders can follow it. Two significant advantages of a team-member selection process that is based on individual roles are, first, team leaders have a process for recruiting the best possible people to fulfill the objectives assigned to the team. Second, management has a process it must support, including but not limited to budgeting for the resources needed to complete the process.

Team leaders must be able to count on receiving adequate time and resources to follow the organization's team-member-selection process. With a management-backed effort, there is a high probability that the team-selection process will succeed the first time around.

6

Challenge 4: Building Trust Among Team Members

Many team leaders attempt to build a "dream team." Unfortunately, most dream teams fail. For example, the 2004 U.S. Olympic men's basketball team, made up entirely of NBA stars and heralded as The Dream Team, finished third after losing to Lithuania. The Dream Team did not fail for lack of skill. It failed for numerous reasons, but perhaps the most damaging is that, as "stars," the egotistical players were concerned more about their individual opportunities for glory than about the success of the team.

Refusing to trust one another, the NBA players failed to commit to becoming a "team." Trust is fundamental to a winning team. If team members do not trust one another, they will be preoccupied with watching their own backs and cannot be successful at working together. Team members who distrust other team members suspect they are withholding information, stretching the truth, or trying to get credit for specific tasks.

Another U.S. Olympic team had a different experience. Coached by the inspirational Herb Brooks, the ice hockey team that beat the Soviet Union in Lake Placid, New York, consisted entirely of college players and was built on the concept of maximizing team chemistry. When selecting players for his team, Brooks focused on finding not the best players but players who could put aside rivalries and personal glory to build powerful team trust.

Ask yourself whether you trust your boss. If you do not, you are probably reluctant to tell him or her about serious problems. Without trust, you probably end up hiding problems instead of working to correct them. One project leader I interviewed expressed the sentiment thusly: "Why would I tell my boss when the possibility always exists that I could die before he finds out about the problem?"

Consider your own integrity: The way and degree to which we trust others, institutions, and organizations can reveal our innermost strengths and weaknesses in terms of our ability to work successfully on a team. Ask yourself the following:

- Would I tell a colleague he is not treating me fairly?
- Would I report someone stealing merchandise to the store manager?
- Would I report an organization's improper but not necessarily illegal accounting practices to authorities?
- Would I tell my boss I thought she made an error in judgment?

If you answered no to any of these questions, you probably fear the potential outcome and do not trust that, despite demonstrating moral turpitude, you will be treated fairly.

Putting the "I" into Building Trust Among Team Members

To me, putting the "I" into building trust in teamwork suggests something infinite that must be built over time. To make the concept of trust tangible, many organizations use simple, adaptable, trust-building exercises. In one, a person falls backward into the presumably outstretched arms of a potential teammate. The exercise vividly demonstrates the need for teammates to trust in each other. Trust must be built over time by a team leader whose intent it is to assure team success.

Typical Approach to Building Trust Among Team Members

Trust creates the chemistry that enables openness among team members who are willing to work together to accomplish the team objective. It is not the same as *consensus*, which comes about only when team members agree on an approach or recommendation. With a decision reached by consensus, a team member may express support while inwardly disagreeing. People who support a consensus decision but do not agree with it may disagree for any number of reasons. The person may not want to fight for an alternative decision. He or she may not believe that the decision is the correct one but feels reluctant to own accountability for the team decision. Unfortunately, in certain circumstances, a person may show support for the consensus decision while planning to take subsequent action that will result in team failure.

Consensus does not require trust. Sometimes, teams reach consensus because it is the *popular* rather than the *right* thing to do. In such instances, people fairly trip over themselves to distance themselves from a consensus action once that action begins to fail.

World–Class Approach to Building Trust Among Team Members

The U.S. Marine Corps builds a group of men and women whose lives depend on their trust in one another. Each recruit drills to do the right thing—whether or not the action is best for the individual. Such auto-response performance is essential in war, particularly in combat, for reasons that need no further explanation. All Marines know that their own and their colleagues' lives depend on being able to trust one another.

At boot camp at Parris Island, North Carolina, one activity drilled into men and women training to become Marines is referred to as "Two Sheets and a Blanket." It goes like this: Each recruit receives a blanket and sheets along with the order to make his or her bed in three minutes. The first time recruits practice this activity, some finish the exercise, stand at attention, and wait for the three minutes to end. Recruits who fail to make their bed in three minutes know what to expect next: screaming, from red-faced drill sergeants. But most people are unprepared for the discovery that *everyone* is a target for the sergeants' wrath. *Everyone's* bed must be made within three minutes. The lesson recruits quickly learn is that everyone fails if just one fails, that all members of the team must pass muster or all will fail together.

World-class teams understand the concept behind the boot-camp drill, and devote necessary time and resources to building trust among team members. Five best practices to build team trust follow.

Five Building–Team–Trust Best Team Practices

- *Building-Trust Process Best Team Practice 1: Develop and endorse a team Code of Ethics.*

Advocating a team Code of Ethics may sound formal and time-consuming, but it can and should be straightforward and easy to accomplish. A team Code of Ethics is simply a list of team-activity tasks and concepts that team members agree to uphold. The code may endorse everyone's willingness, for example, to listen to any proposal. It may require keeping what is said in committee meetings confidential or helping other team members to complete assignments. It could condemn taking credit for team activities not participated in or criticizing individuals, whether teammates or outsiders. One item every team Code of Ethics should include is the stipulation that everyone arrive promptly for team meetings, participate enthusiastically in team activities, and complete individual assignments effectively and efficiently.

The 1980 U.S. Olympic gold-medal hockey team provides an optimal trust-building model for all teams to follow. However, it is unrealistic to expect that what happened to that team can be replicated by every business team, and it is particularly unlikely to be feasible for teams with members who either covertly or overtly avoid working for the benefit of the team. Developing a Code of Ethics and pledging to follow it for the duration of team activities is a way to define expectations for all team members.

A team with one or more individual members who do not want to sign or follow the Code of Ethics can expect trouble. Clearly, a team of four colleagues working harmoniously together is light-years more effective than a team of five people, one of whom—for whatever reason—does not want to be on the team.

An organization may choose to standardize a team Code of Ethics for all employees or it may opt to develop a code tailored to each specific activity. Typically, organizations that support a team Code of Ethics standardize a code to be used company-wide with no or few modifications. Such standardization relieves team leaders of one task and indicates that management supports a team Code of Ethics.

- *Building-Trust Process Best Team Practice 2: Walk the talk.*

Corporate-speak defines how management expresses itself regarding corporate governance practices as "tone at the top." Management shows esteem for or disapproval of specific business practices as well as for its employees, customers, and suppliers by its tone at the top. A corporation's tone at the top begins with the chief executive officer and board of directors and flows down to every level of management. As a member of management, a team leader needs to toe the party line and "walk the talk." Unless they intend to commit political suicide, team leaders should enact the tone at the top, follow and enforce the team Code of Ethics, and model how they would like their team to function. Management talk of what is appropriate and ethical behavior must be manifest in all managers' actions.

- *Building-Trust Process Best Team Practice 3: Select a trustworthy assistant leader for the team.*

Corporate history evidences that a key ingredient for team success is a leader's very loyal assistant. A leader normally receives most of the limelight and credit for success while his or her assistant works behind the scenes. A loyal assistant should be willing to apprise a leader of any actual or anticipated problems.

One example of how such a partnership should work is the team of Michael Eisner and Frank Wells, who for several decades ran Walt Disney Company. At the time Michael Eisner became CEO, Disney was floundering but, in a relatively short period of time, he and Frank Wells engineered a remarkable turnaround. Under their leadership, the company enjoyed phenomenal success until being brought to a halt when Frank Wells died in a helicopter crash. The power of the partnership ended, and Michael Eisner alone was unable to achieve the results their partnership had generated.

Building trust among team members requires a foundation of trust as well as strong chemistry between a team leader and his or her top assistant. One of the first decisions a team leader should make is whom to appoint. I advise team leaders to choose an assistant whose skills, work ethic, and personal and professional preferences are well known. Selecting someone with whom they have both worked extensively and enjoyed good chemistry and mutual trust is essential for team success. For some team leaders, an additional requirement might be someone who is willing to remain discreetly in the shadows to let the leader receive all the glory.

- *Building-Trust Process Best Team Practice 4: Reward good work— whether it results in success or failure.*

During years working with large corporations, I came to the conclusion that some people drive into the company parking lot, stash their brains in the glove compartment, work mindlessly all day until returning to their car to reinsert their brains, and then drive away to accomplish wonderful things. The philosophy behind this behavior? "If you don't do anything, you can't do anything wrong."

Rewarding good work even when the result is failure is a proven concept adopted by many businesses. In fact, back in the early days of IBM, a senior vice president in charge of a project costing more than one million dollars experienced a complete project failure. With flames still raging at the conclusion of the project, the CEO called the manager into his office. Assuming he would be fired for the failure, the manager decided to take matters into his own hands and asked the CEO whether he was out of a job. The surprising reply: "No. I have just invested a million dollars training you—I can't afford to fire you."

Two important reasons why organizations should reward good work that fails are that reward encourages people to take risks because they know that if they fail they won't be punished, and that reward encourages people to report anticipated failure, ideally in time for problems to be corrected. If all failure is punished and reasonable risk-taking is not rewarded, team members may withhold critical information from their management, further endangering a project.

More and more organizations realize the benefits of rewarding legitimate failure. For example, in one very small organization, a person's minor failure was analyzed over a free cup of coffee. A major failure that resulted from someone having taken a risk was rewarded with an all-expenses-paid dinner for the risk-taker and her spouse.

Rewards do not have to be elaborate—they just need to

encourage rational risk-taking. By rewarding risk-taking and acknowledging that risky approaches may fail, organizations build and support conditions that also may provide a real productivity breakthrough. Clearly, a team leader must differentiate between failure due to legitimate risk-taking and failure due to carelessness or incompetence, neither of which should ever earn reward.

- *Building-Trust Process Best Team Practice 5: Select the "right" team members, those whose chemistry fits the team, not necessarily the most skilled.*

Facilitating team-member trust and chemistry are more important than putting together a team of the most qualified people. Dream-team members may possess superior skills but they often lack the chemistry or the selflessness necessary to gel with their teammates.

One process to evaluate potential team-member chemistry assesses people according to four roles:

- The individual wants to *make it happen* and is eager to be team leader.
- The individual wants to *help it happen* and is willing to do whatever is necessary to assure team success.
- The individual wants to *let it happen* and, although somewhat indifferent about team objectives, will not try to undermine team assignments.
- The individual wants to *stop it from happening* and, although he or she seems to support team activities, behaves behind the scenes in dramatically different fashion.

Team leaders should recruit as many team members who want to *help* make it happen as possible. Then, by combining people who will work for team success with people who embody the "let it happen" ethic, leaders can use the team dynamic to motivate the laissez-faire individuals, with the ultimate goal being their "conversion" to become "help it happen" types. Willing, competent individuals who can bond with other team members to develop a winning chemistry are the right people for almost any team.

Impediments to the Building-Team-Trust Challenge

Two impediments to creating trust between team members arise when no previous working relationship exists that supports trust and when an atmosphere of distrust results from previous interactions. In the first scenario, one can easily understand that it can be difficult for individuals to trust a team leader or teammates with whom they have no work relationship. Initial disinclination to trust combined with the need to develop trust over time is a significant hurdle at the start of a project. Without experiencing even small fulfillments of trust, team members' skills and competencies may not be enough for the team to complete project goals.

In the case of distrust due to past interactions with team members or team leaders—whether based on experience, misperceived behavior, or irrational dislike—emotional baggage will interfere with people's ability to perform successfully. For example, if a person works on a team with someone who promotes himself or herself unfairly, the person understandably may distrust the other person's motives and may be unwilling to share knowledge or to work diligently.

Strategies to Overcome the Building-Team-Trust Challenge

Two long-term strategies that help build trust are doing what you say you will do and encouraging open discussion of problems from the past. Team leaders should be specific about team activities and accomplishments. Setting an example by explicitly fulfilling promises, team leaders can emphasize their trustworthiness. A team leader who announces, for example, that a meeting will end at 3:00 PM and, in fact, does end the meeting at the promised time builds trust. Stating and delivering on small promises may not build an unbreakable relationship quickly, but the practice should reduce distrust.

Open discussion of prior events that caused distrust provides another strong bridge. When someone on a team, say, appears to take credit for another team member's work, the action may or may not be intentional but it causes distrust. What matters most in resolving such feelings so that they do not simmer from the beginning of team activities to the end is open, blameless discussion.

Team leaders need to initiate these discussions in order to make all people aware of what is acceptable behavior.

Building–Team–Trust Plan of Action

Team leaders can build trust following a two-part plan of action. The first step is for team leaders to recognize the importance of trust to team success. Leaders who naively believe teams can work effectively when team members do not trust one another may be doomed to fail. While great chemistry between all team members may not be possible, a basic level of trust is necessary if members of a team are going to work together to accomplish a team objective.

The second step is to exemplify (and make explicit) trust-building actions. Authorizing responsibility to and trusting in a second-in-command is one way a team leader can exhibit the benefits of developing trust. By emphasizing consistent fulfillment of small goals and rewarding rational risk-taking, leaders also help teams learn to trust their own skills and ability to succeed.

A bonus best practice for building trust among team members is to keep intact teams that succeed. Teams often succeed because team members trust each other. If a new team recruits several or all individuals from a previously successful team, the probability of its success significantly increases. While this strategy may not be practical in the long term for some organizations, a core group of team members from a successful team may build into another successful team.

7

Challenge 5: Training Team Members to Accomplish Their Assignments

Growing up, I had a dog that followed me everywhere and showered me with love. I called him Roderique the Wonder Dog and I thought him the best dog in the neighborhood. When he was a puppy, I planned how to teach him to shake hands, sit up on his hind legs and beg, and roll over—all the basic tricks.

Roderique the Wonder Dog was always eager to please me but initially he seemed confused about what I wanted him to do. So, I would show him by miming the trick and then speaking the command. As he learned, I rewarded him with treats for doing a trick correctly. Slowly, over time, I trained him to do what I wanted.

When my wife and I became parents, we repeated a version of this process with our children. The tricks and rewards were different, but the process was fundamentally the same. If I wanted my daughter to behave in a certain way, I had to train her. My wife and I continued using this process as our children grew, spending countless hours teaching them to read, swim, ride a bike, play tennis, and, eventually, to drive a car. Training them involved an investment of our time, of course, but the investment was well rewarded.

Are people on teams any different? Do team members naturally know how to behave as members of a team? Do team members intuitively know how to perform each task assigned to them? Do team members know exactly what is expected from them? The answer to most of these questions is no, and, for that reason, an organization desiring fully functional, effective teams must train and equip team members to perform its mission.

Putting the "I" into Training Team Members

Organizations and team leaders should not attempt to train individual team members—the "I" in teams—until those individuals can demonstrate that they are able and willing to perform necessary tasks, and that they meet the team's entrance criteria. Individuals need to be trained and they need to be appropriately prepared and equipped in order to fulfill team responsibilities.

Just as individual members of a baseball or football team must be coached as they begin preseason training, individual members of newly formed business teams must be coached. In sports, individual players work to build muscle, dexterity, and endurance, training their mind and body to perform essential skills relative to the position they play. A pitcher, say, may be assigned to a special training area for the afternoon to pitch to a target. A football center may be directed to practice drills hiking a ball to a receiver.

Practices that seem logical for sports teams translate wonderfully to business teams. Unfortunately, however, many organizations do not invest necessary time and money in training and equipping individuals for teamwork. Their management erroneously assumes individuals are qualified to perform teamwork because they graduated from university or were given high marks during the hiring process. These factors, although important in the selection decision-making process, are not reliable indicators of teamwork skills.

Although many educational institutions reward students for the assignments they accomplish working alone, few evaluate the work accomplished by several individuals who combine to form a team, and fewer still give team tests. As a result, most people begin work on a team with a bias, expecting that their individual accomplishments will be rewarded and that they will not be rewarded solely based on the combined efforts of the team. To counter this bias, leaders need to train people to think about work in terms of the team as a whole before commencing teamwork. This training is especially critical if an organization is to build a world-class team.

Typical Approach to Training Team Members

In addition to training and equipping individual team members fully, organizations must also commit resources to teaching *team leaders* how to fulfill their responsibilities. A leader who may be responsible, for example, for helping develop consensus among team members needs to know how to accomplish this goal.

Some organizations expedite training by placing a skilled facilitator on the team. Generally, a facilitator does not work with team members to complete tasks, but rather teaches members how to work together. The facilitator helps team members develop basic team dynamics but does not have a real say in team decisions. A facilitator who knows consensus techniques, for example, can help a team learn and apply them. He or she should never be cast in the role of team leader, but instead should serve as a kind of teacher with a specialized set of skills.

World–Class Approach to Training Team Members

Ideally, individuals assigned to a team have the following goals: to fulfill their responsibilities to the utmost, to contribute without reservation to the team's success, and to earn reward for their work. If a team is properly trained and achieves its goals, its success should be rewarded. Regardless of team success, successful team members should be rewarded.

Reward does not necessarily involve direct, fiscal compensation. Diverse forms of reward can motivate and satisfy team members, with many individuals happy to work in hope of individual praise or special recognition for their own or their team's contribution. Others may work to receive the praise and respect of their colleagues, a reward often more highly coveted than money. Whatever motivations operate behind the scenes, training is the secret ingredient. Implement the five practices below to contribute to training team members.

Five Training–Team–Members Best Team Practices

- *Training-Team-Members Process Best Team Practice 1: Separate team success from individual success.*

Tom Landry, the winningest coach of the Dallas Cowboys, attributed much of his success to his approach to responsibility and reward. As previously noted, Landry assumed full credit or blame whether the team won or lost, but he held players individually responsible for performing the mission for which each had been trained. Landry justified this approach by ensuring in advance through repetitive drills that every player was adequately trained to the rigors of the mission.

Landry understood the direct relationship between training, preparation, and reward, seeing to it that a trainee who performed by rote perfection earned reward. Rewarding individuals based on team success triangulates and distances incentives from work. An able trainee may choose not to expend skill, for example, if the potential failure of the team may negate his efforts to earn reward. Landry assigned each member of the Dallas Cowboys specific goals and objectives to accomplish. Under Landry, the team could lose, but individual players nevertheless could receive reward. Landry also recognized an individual team member's poor contribution to the team's win—even when the team won by a large margin—by penalizing individual team members who did not meet goals and objectives.

Business teams also need to define individual goals and objectives—as well as rewards for accomplishing them—and team goals and objectives for which all team members share in the success. Just as five defensive-line football players may earn a reward if they prevent, say, the sacking of their quarterback for at least ten seconds after a hike, so may individual business team members benefit upon the team's overall success. The message here is clear: Reward group success *in addition to* rewarding individual success—not in lieu of it.

- *Training-Team-Members Process Best Team Practice 2: Objectively define individual team members' responsibilities.*

People need to know their specific responsibilities on the job as well as the particulars their supervisors will consider when evaluating their work. In my early days when I worked for one or another large corporation, I always felt I had three jobs. The first matched the job description; the second entailed work I actually performed (this frequently differed from tasks specified in the job description); the third was meeting my supervisor's evaluation criteria. If I were smart enough to identify all evaluation criteria in order to focus my effort on doing the third job as well as possible, I generally could lock in a good performance appraisal. Unfortunately, some of the criteria were not quantifiable, such as my manners during a working lunch with my manager or whether I behaved appropriately while attending the boss's wedding.

Individuals cannot earn individual reward unless their assigned tasks are measurable. For example, if a team leader asks someone to take minutes at the team's weekly status meetings, the leader must provide the person with objective, measurable criteria with which he or she will judge the quality of the minutes. Necessary components could include meeting date and time, attendee names and areas of specialization, items discussed, and decisions tabled or made. One measurement a supervisor might take into consideration is whether all meeting attendees agree that the minutes include all pertinent information.

At some point or other during your career or even during your school years, you probably found yourself on a team with one or more people who did nothing. They did not participate in job-specific conversations; they did not perform assigned tasks; they did not offer suggestions or take a stand. When teamwork finishes, many organizations reward all team members equally, providing, say, a night on the town for those who did nothing as well as for those who did the bulk of the work. Is this fair or unfair?

Well, how an organization chooses to reward or penalize is that organization's prerogative, but you can make fairness your standard by objectively identifying individual team members' responsibilities and tasks via written, precisely defined job descriptions. Descriptions must be specific enough that individuals know without the shadow of a doubt what they will be held responsible for. By referring to written job descriptions, team leaders can objectively assess whether or not an individual completes assigned work.

- *Training-Team-Members Process Best Team Practice 3: Develop and implement a training plan for each team member.*

As every professional sports coach knows, a comprehensive training plan is essential to a winning team. To develop a training plan for a business team, the team leader must first identify what skills a project will demand and then determine where team members lack proficiency. Once necessary skills and candidates to train are identified, the team leader can plan activities and a timetable for training that are contingent upon project scheduling and budget.

In some cases, the team leader or another member of the team can teach team members the skills to complete certain tasks. In other cases, trainees can attend a seminar or class offered by a third-party vendor. A third option is to adapt to project challenges as they occur rather than identifying and planning for training in advance of need. Regardless of the approach, team leaders should identify each member's skill set to prepare for training and skills supplementation.

- *Training-Team-Members Process Best Team Practice 4: Supplement and support individual team members' completion of individual and team tasks.*

When my daughter was very young, she wanted to ride a two-wheel bicycle. Some of her friends were already riding two-wheelers, but I worried that if she fell and got hurt, she would not want to get back on the bike.

In time, she made it abundantly clear that her tricycle would no longer do, and so, like any good parent, I helped her up onto the seat of a brand-new two-wheeler, grabbed hold, and ran alongside as she pedaled. While this was a strenuous task for me, she did not fall and, over time, became more confident riding the bike. My next step was to take my hand off the seat while she rode. Of course, I ran alongside so that if she began to fall, I could catch her. My objective was that she would not lose confidence in riding her two-wheeler because of a frightening fall.

Team leaders can be similarly protective in an effort to prevent team members from "falling." Faced with a situation in which a leader knows something will not work, most will say something rather than just stand by and watch the assignment fail. Failure of that sort should not happen in team activities.

The same willingness to intervene must reside in team members. If members work as a team and care about other team members, they should not want another to fail. Team members should step in and offer advice, work with each other, or even cooperate with a struggling team member to complete a task. Deciding how to perform a task can take the form of consensus or mandate. Imagine a case in which you have already determined how you will complete a task when your colleagues suggest alternatives. Do you say to yourself, *It's my task and I'll do it my way*, or do you take the advice and accept criticism as well-intended? Good team members learn how to argue for their own way as well as to benefit from a broadening horizon through discussion. However, they must fine-tune their radar to recognize a better way when they come upon one.

- *Training-Team-Members Process Best Team Practice 5: Appoint a quality-control coach for the team.*

As I have noted elsewhere, I first met Tom Landry at a charity event. As we discussed our professions, I explained that I was involved in information quality assurance. Landry's reply surprised me as he remarked that, although most people attending the event knew him as the coach of the Dallas Cowboys, he also considered himself "an industrial engineer and a big supporter of the quality philosophy."

One of the innovations Landry introduced to the Cowboys was a quality-control coach. At the time, this was a new concept in football. The quality-control coach sat high in the stands and watched the team execute plays. He knew how the team should perform plays and could identify when an individual team member failed to fulfill his responsibility. The quality-control coach could also recognize situations in which certain plays would not work.

The legendary quality-assurance pioneer W. Edwards Deming clarified and classified *quality* in manufacturing while participating in the Hawthorne experiments that were conducted in Cicero, Illinois, at Western Electric, in the nineteen-twenties and thirties. Discussing the cause of variation in the quality of manufactured goods, Deming named two culprits: *common cause* and *special cause*. A variation in quality occurs as the result of "common" cause when the process is not carried out as specified. A variation results from a "special" cause when some factor from outside of the normal environment intervenes. In football, for example, if a play intended to run a ball through the center of a defensive line fails, thereby varying from planned success, the cause of variation is common and the quality-control coach would try to determine why. If the plan fails because the opposing center weighs 375 pounds and is unusually quick on his feet, the cause would be special.

Every business team needs a quality-control coach— someone who can observe the team's performance and determine when and why work is not progressing correctly. If due to a common cause, perhaps a team member lacks a needed skill. If due to a special cause, perhaps a powerful executive opposes a team's proposed solution. Team leaders then need to find other solutions and ways of working toward project goals. Compromise is a key characteristic of team success.

Impediments to the Training–Team–Members Challenge

As would be presumed from earlier discussions, organizations face numerous obstacles to training team members. Team members, for example, may not want to be on a team and therefore fight the idea of team-specific training. Many team members believe they are selected because they are subject-matter experts or because they represent a specific area or job responsibility. However, most team members do not recognize that being a master of team dynamics helps fulfill their role. They may think they have higher-priority assignments than those associated with the team. They may even balk because they suspect they will not be given enough time to learn all skills and techniques necessary for fulfilling their assignments. Reasons such as these are common and can be devastating to team success.

When, for example, a person does not want to be a member of a team, the organization wastes time and money trying to train him or her to become an effective team member. During my days as a coach for my son's Little League baseball team, I recognized that some kids went out for the team because their fathers wanted them to participate. The kids themselves did not want to be on the team, and spent most of their time gazing at the clouds and picking dandelions. If I had expended time and effort trying to train them, it probably would not have contributed to the team's success.

Most probably, attempting to train these kids would have afflicted them with unwarranted stress. Although I sometimes regret not putting more effort into attempting to train them (because my attention could have converted some kids who thought they did not want to play on a team, but whose resistance perhaps was the result of issues with a father figure or some other factor unrelated to teams or baseball), I did what I thought best at the time and trained kids who *wanted* training.

Team processes, whether implemented in Little League or Big Business America, are interrelated. If the team-member-selection process is defective, individuals who do not want to participate in team activities end up on teams. The failure lies not in those individuals' *training* but in their *selection* as team members.

Many people cannot complete their primary job assignments in forty hours a week and must work evenings and weekends without extra pay. Piling on team assignments takes additional time away from employees' personal lives. It is up to the team leader and the individual's supervisor to persuade him or her of the benefits of team participation and team-specific training.

I know personally how tough it can be to persuade someone assigned unwillingly to a team to prioritize training for team assignments while he or she is pressured by a direct supervisor to complete primary job tasks. I know because it happened to me more than once. At one particular job, when I was young and blind to the politics at play, I would prepare to leave my office to go to a team training meeting and my supervisor would remind me that I would need to make up lost time to complete my day-to-day assignments. I faced a tough choice: either to do my regular work at night or on the weekend, or to skip team training meetings and ignore team assignments. As I was young and green, hoping to get ahead, and working under a supervisor solely responsible for my performance appraisal, I made up the time as best I could and did what my supervisor wanted. Had I been more experienced, I would have directly addressed the conflict with my supervisor and the team leader in order to get my assignments for both done on paid time instead of Perry time.

Strategies to Overcome the Training–Team–Members Challenge

To overcome impediments to providing adequate team-member training, organizations can force supervisors to release their subordinates to train to perform team activities. Organizations may also mandate that supervisors work with team leaders to establish assignment priorities based on realistic estimates of whatever time and resources will be needed for training.

When a determination is made that a specific individual can be trained to become an ideal team member, that individual's supervisor must hear cogent, compelling reasons why the person was selected and how much time he or she will need to spend training. The supervisor must also know how the activities of the team can benefit the company as a whole as well as his or her department. Convincing a supervisor usually is necessary before he or she will allow a subordinate time to train. The supervisor may also need to be persuaded to reduce the subordinate's workload.

Team leaders need to work with an individual's supervisor to reach mutual consent regarding priority of assignments. For team leaders to be confident of a supervisor's approval of a training schedule, they need to get agreement in advance and then prioritize certain team activities over normal work assignments. They must also develop relationships with supervisors that allow the leader and supervisor to jointly prioritize work. Even before seeking a supervisor's consent regarding a training schedule, team leaders must realistically estimate resources and calendar time for training. If the organization will not allocate the needed amount of time, the team leader may choose to dissolve the team rather than attempt a task it cannot successfully complete, or he or she may opt to reduce the mission to tasks the team can accomplish without additional training.

Training–Team–Members Plan of Action

A team leader and all team members must treat each other as unique individuals, recognizing each other's strengths and weaknesses, to truly work effectively. A team-training plan of action should include the following steps:

- Step 1: Know each other's preferences and peeves.
- Step 2: Conduct team-building exercises.

The team leader and all team members must get to know each other as individuals. People do not have to like each other, but they do need to be able to work together to achieve common goals. Knowing what other members of the team like or dislike, consider good or bad experiences, and view as their strengths or weaknesses powerfully affects whether team activities succeed.

For example, people on a team are not just analysts or developers; they are whole entities with complex preferences and personalities and often are products of distinctly different cultural, geographical, and racial environments. Generational differences also factor into a person's makeup. These diverse characteristics express themselves in the way people approach teamwork and present ideas, and in the type of training they expect.

Members need to develop rapport before a team can begin working toward fulfilling its mission. To establish a healthy team ethos even before training begins, a leader may need to put people together in a room to interact for an hour or to immerse them for a day or two of sole commitment to coming together as a team.

Team leaders can aid team rapport by engaging people in activities that motivate them to work together as a unit. Team-building activities can be as simple as having people sit around a table, taking turns describing their experience and background, or as formal as sending people offsite to special camps that conduct exercises designed to create a cohesive, interdependent group from a motley crew.

8

Challenge 6: Listening to the Voice of the Customer

A person cannot listen to the voice of the customer until he or she knows who the customer is. A developer, when conceiving of a complex product, probably cannot visualize the full spate of potential customers or even whether satisfying their requirements is more important than satisfying those of organizational management. Many teams become hamstrung trying to please too many parties or failing to recognize which party would be essential to please.

Take, for example, the true story of an insurance company's IT group, mandated to build an information system for use by independent insurance agents. The IT project team assumed that a "department" within an insurance company was its customer. Therefore, team members interacted with this department, gathered specifications for the software from it, and built the system according to its specs. When the system was operational, the independent insurance agents were aghast. The system was not agent-friendly to independents spread across the globe, did not do what they needed, and was unresponsive to the requests of individual agents, making it difficult for them to close sales with their customers. If the IT project team had recognized that independent agents spread across the globe were the customers, not a single-site department, it would have built an entirely different system.

A mistake organizations make over and over is building a product the customer doesn't want. Bankruptcies flourish because organizations think that if they build a "better" product, customers will flock to buy it. Very often, exactly the opposite happens. One only needs to skim a hundred-page-plus cell-phone manual to know that manufacturers incorporate many more features in their products than a customer will ever use. Teams need to know who their customers are, and then they need to listen to them.

Putting the "I" into Listening to the Voice of the Customer

For the "I" in this challenge, we need only look to individual software users. I remember attending a conference at which fellow IT professionals almost unanimously agreed that software users—not analysts or developers—were responsible for their own dissatisfaction with software products. In truth, many systems analysts believe they know better what users need than do users themselves.

The trick is to identify the true customer among many potential customers for products and services recommended by development teams. There are different types of customers, with different needs. Teams need to hear the various voices and then make decisions about what will provide the greatest satisfaction to most customers.

Teams cannot always meet with every potential customer. Listening to the voice of the customer means that individual team members need to gather requirements from many different customers. In the independent-insurance-agent fiasco, IT learned the hard lesson that it needed to differentiate between the internal customer, the external customer, and the distant customer.

Teams must identify as many customers for a planned product as possible, as well as the type of information they need from each customer. For example, if an external agent in the insurance-software scenario requested a specific function, the development team would need to identify who would pay for that functionality. Keeping such a request in mind, team members then can decide who on the team is best qualified to listen to that customer's voice, and report information back for team discussion.

Typical Approach to Listening to the Voice of the Customer

Most product designers and service providers are order-takers. They function as waiters or waitresses in a restaurant: They wait for a customer to tell them what he or she wants to eat. Things get more complicated when the customer wants a type of cuisine, say

Italian or French, rather than a specific appetizer or entrée to be ordered by name.

In many parts of the world, restaurants post a No Substitutions notice. If a diner is allergic to an ingredient in a specific dish, he or she must try to find a different selection that doesn't contain the ingredient. The No Substitutions philosophy seems to be, "We do what we do. If you're not satisfied, go somewhere else"—and many people do. Of course, there is another possible reason for the No Substitutions policy. It could be that all dishes are prepared offsite or in advance. All the restaurant staff does is reheat, as needed, and serve; it cannot remove an ingredient already blended in.

Both of these possibilities can apply to teams because many team members function only as order-takers. Management assigns work, dictating the type of product or service a team is to produce. Teams don't know who the customers are, and if they did, they quite possibly wouldn't listen very carefully.

World–Class Approach to Listening to the Voice of the Customer

Many organizations post signs they presume employees will internalize, emphasizing the following:

- The customer is always right.
- Our goal is to exceed customer expectations.
- Without the customer, you would not have a job.

These banalities ignore myriad conflicts between customers of a product. A less terse, but incredibly more valuable, posting might read something like the following:

- Customers are always right about their desires, but not necessarily about their needs or their capacity to have those needs met in a particular form.

World-class teams incorporate the idea of listening to the customer in their development process. If we expand our definition of "customer" and phrase it in terms of the example of the independent insurance agents, we might find that customers also include people in the following categories:

- members of management that authorized the team
- team members' supervisors
- the legal department
- the accounting department
- internal auditors
- quality-control personnel

To pay heed to the voice of the customer, one assumes that the customer has precisely articulated what he or she wants. Most customers know what they want but many have difficulty describing it, in part because they don't know the process by which their needs will be met. Understanding the voice of the customer requires good listening skills, which include assuring that the team hears what the customer says.

Consider, for example, an experience I had not long ago when I needed to buy a new lawn mower. The first salesperson I intercepted mid-stride at my local home-and-garden supply store hurriedly told me that the store carried many different styles for each of three brands of lawn mower, all on display at the back of the store, and then asked, "Which one do you want?" Since I wasn't sure, I said I'd just walk around and look at the choices.

Before I'd even reached the mowers, a second salesperson asked whether I needed help. She looked ready to listen, so I told her I needed a new lawn mower. As she walked with me toward the back of the store, she asked questions about the size of my yard, the terrain, whether there were rocks and trees, and so on. When we got to the mowers, she took me straight to one, saying, "This could do the trick. It has a rear grass-bag so you won't be bumping the bag into trees, and it has enough power and size to cut your lawn in a reasonable amount of time."

Which salesperson do you think was experienced at listening to the voice of the customer? By asking relevant questions, the saleswoman was able to close the sale in just a few minutes, demonstrating what listening to the voice of the customer actually means.

The following five practices can help teams better understand how to identify and listen to the voice of the customer and ensure that team results meet the true needs of users.

Five Voice-of-the-Customer Best Team Practices

- *Listening–to-the-Voice-of-the-Customer Process Best Team Practice 1: Ask the customer for acceptance criteria.*

A team needs to know how the customer will determine whether the results of the team effort are usable. "Acceptance criteria" define the tangibles and intangibles that will meet the needs of the customer. In meeting these criteria, the team will have met the needs of the customer and thus have listened to—and satisfied—the voice of the customer.

Many customers state that although they may not be able to define exactly what they want, they will know it when they see it. A team's job is to translate details about "know it when they see it" into acceptance criteria. For example, if I were to begin today to build a home from the foundation up, I probably wouldn't know much about electrical work, but I would know that when I move in, I would want to be able to turn lights on and off. I know that I would want to be able to come into the kitchen through the garage and be able to turn on the kitchen overhead at the garage door. I know that I would want to be able to turn on high-hat lights as I enter the bedroom. My acceptance criteria—light fixtures and on-off switches where I want them—provide an electrician with crucial information to design a system to satisfy my wishes.

Some organizations develop predefined acceptance criteria to jump-start this process. These include such factors as cost, availability, usability, changeability, training materials, and ongoing support. While generalized lists do not cover all possible acceptance criteria, they help customers think in terms of what the product or service must be in order to be acceptable to them.

- *Listening–to-the-Voice-of-the-Customer Process Best Team Practice 2: Conduct customer surveys throughout all phases of the project.*

A survey is a process in which a customer is asked to answer specific questions about a product or service he or she will use.

Surveys can be submitted to customers in writing or orally in person or over the telephone. Many organizations use easy-to-complete e-mail surveys.

A survey is an information-gathering instrument. Even when completed with seemingly precise requirements, the survey will not represent the full voice of the customer if it was prepared by the group developing the product for the customer because that group's concept of what the customer wants will bias the questions the group asks. To encourage customers to include information not specifically requested, the survey should provide blank sections and sufficient time for the customer to answer in detail.

Survey questions should be phrased so as to elicit precisely worded responses. A survey that asks the customer whether he or she wants a bell or a whistle on the widget gathers more-useful information than one that asks whether features are desired. Survey questions should be worded in such a way that customers can answer them without a lot of effort, and so that people analyzing the responses do not need to spend an inordinate amount of time trying to decipher what the customer intended.

Teams can modify a boilerplate survey to gather different kinds of information at various times during a project. During the requirements-gathering period, a survey can serve as a data-collection document to help the team define acceptance criteria. Modified midway through the project, it can be used to help team members determine whether work is on track to meet objectives, or whether they need to adjust the process. Administered after delivery of the product or service, a survey can help team members evaluate whether the product or service meets customer needs. If it does not, the survey can help team members focus additional work.

- *Listening–to-the-Voice-of-the-Customer Process Best Team Practice 3: Ensure that teams visit customer worksites to observe work firsthand.*

To appreciate the challenges customers face, team members need to walk in their shoes. A visit to a customer site allows team members to observe firsthand the work practices and preferences of that customer. In some instances, it may be enough to just sit, watch, and listen to what goes on. In other instances, a team member might follow the flow of work as it enters a customer site, then is processed, and finally is delivered as a product or service to an external customer.

Many team members rate visits to customer sites among their most valuable professional experiences. It is difficult to know, for example, exactly how your customer's warehouse works if you have never been inside it. In most cases, team leaders and members need to do more than simply observe the scene; they must read every manual, discuss the mission with every accommodating manager and staff member, and gather every bit of information from every conceivable source.

- *Listening–to-the-Voice-of-the-Customer Process Best Team Practice 4: Conduct focus groups with customer participation.*

Customers can pair with a facilitator to form a focus group. In some commercial focus groups, participants sit behind a one-way glass and observe customers as they describe what they want in the delivered product.

Team members generally should neither plan nor sit in on a customer focus group, which should be conducted by a trained facilitator with no vested interest in the customer or the team. Properly trained facilitators enable and empower focus group participants to express their true feelings. Removing fear and expectation from the equation frees people to share their opinions and needs.

The team should receive and analyze results after the conclusion of focus group activities. Results may be provided to the team in the form of an informal set of notes, an audiotape of the focus group's discussion, or a written, formal report from the facilitator. It is important that the team not criticize customers for what they communicate in a focus group. Team members may discuss problems with the focus group or request information surfaced by it, but they must avoid attacking a customer as such behavior only discourages trust and renders individuals less willing to constructively identify problems and concerns in the future.

- *Listening–to-the-Voice-of-the-Customer Process Best Team Practice 5: Invite customers to participate in team activities.*

Team members who want to hear the voice of the customer on a regular basis may choose to invite one or more customer representatives to participate on the team. However, they should not invite any customer to participate as a full-time member because full-time participation may cause the person to identify more with the team than with the business area he or she represents. In addition, team members should not invite customers to team meetings held at the onset of a project because customers should not have a say in how the team meets their needs, only in whether it meets them.

Customers participating on a team, like all other team members, need a precisely defined role. For instance, a team may want to limit the customers' role to identifying product requirements. The independent insurance agents described above perhaps should have been limited to expressing requirements directly to the team. They should not have relied on representation by one agency's internal department.

Impediments to the Voice-of-the-Customer Challenge

Sometimes—arguably, *much* of the time—obstacles get in the way of a team's ability to truly listen to the voice of the customer. Perhaps every member of the team is intent on listening but the customer does not know what options are possible in the finished product and therefore does not describe them as requirements. I experienced just this when I looked into purchasing an automobile. I was unaware that satellite radio was an optional feature. If a salesperson had asked me for my exit criteria, I would not have known to include satellite radio. However, as soon as I knew that feature was available, I wanted it. A survey listing optional features would have helped.

Another obstacle might be that team members believe they already know absolutely and positively what the customer needs; therefore, they see no reason to listen to the customer. But listening could result in the team delivering a more satisfactory product.

A third all-too-common problem that demonstrates that team leaders and members are not really listening to the voice of the customer is that, deep down inside, they consider the team's mission to be customer-independent. Unbelievable as it may seem, many teams receive missions that do not include *customer satisfaction*. A team's mission may be to *select* a software accounting system for the customer, which is very different from *developing* an accounting system for use by a specific individual or department. If this team is listening to the voice of the customer, it will understand that it is to survey what is available and then to recommend what it believes is the "best" accounting system for the customer's use.

Strategies to Overcome the Voice–of–the–Customer Challenge

Strategies that help overcome impediments to listening to the voice of the customer include discussing available options with customers, spending time and resources reviewing and meeting with customers, and letting customers know when team members need customer input to shape team assignments. A team's mission should align with its customers' missions. Often, however, customers cannot define their mission because they do not understand the team's capabilities, possible solutions, and methods. Sharing and refining options should be part of the normal dialogue with the customer.

A second strategy is to require that team members both listen *and respond* to the voice of the customer. If a team regularly spends time and resources reviewing a customer's needs and meeting with the customer to discuss identified requirements, it is unlikely to maintain that it knows better than the customer what he or she wants. Every team has a responsibility to meet the needs of the customer as stipulated in the team's mission statement. A strategy to help teams listen to the voice of the customer is to give them clear responsibility and authority to begin interacting with customers. Teams need to inform customers about team activities in which customers have a stake, and they need to provide contact information for customers to communicate their input regarding team assignments.

Voice–of–the–Customer Plan of Action

To help incorporate listening to the customer's voice into their mission, team members can start by identifying the customers for all team activities. Teams assigned a specific task or goal need to know the beneficiaries and users of their work. By listing all customers and stakeholders for all team assignments, teams get a better handle on achieving objectives.

Second, teams should incorporate listening to the voice of the customer into every team assignment. Drawing from the list of customers who will benefit from the team's effort, team members should discuss with the customers what they need in order to fulfill their business responsibilities. This exercise will focus the team's effort on satisfying customers, as opposed to allowing it to put effort into activities that may or may not be on target.

The third strategy involves advising customers in advance of conducting the previously described survey. Team members should tell customers that members of the team will contact them to solicit requirements. Advance notice is advisable because people in most organizations are not encouraged to go up and down the hallways knocking on doors and asking questions— management will need to set the scene for team contact with customers. Team leaders should inform customers, for example, when and through what medium team members will contact them. In addition, they should inform customers how long the surveying process will take, and provide a concise, clear description of benefit to customers and their organization.

9

Challenge 7:
Breaking Down Silos

When Moses led his followers into the desert, they were unorganized—a truly unruly mob. To organize them, Moses conceived of a hierarchical structure many modern businesses copy. A pyramid in shape, this structure has at the top what we today call a president; under the president are vice presidents; next are assistant vice presidents; then come managers, then supervisors, and finally, under the supervisors, there are workers. The hierarchy wrought miracles for Moses, but managers today debate whether what worked for Moses in the desert is the best organizational model for modern businesses.

So what's the debate all about? To find out, let's look at three departments typically found in a simply structured business organization: a purchasing department, an accounting department, and an IT department. Using modern-day jargon, let's call these departmental units *silos*. The management of this hypothetical business expects that each silo will perform its specific activities in the best manner possible. It is notable that, in this and in many businesses, the president—and only the president—has direct authority over the various departments. The accounting department, for example, may report to a controller who reports to the CEO. The IT department may report to a vice president of operations who reports to the CEO. When the IT department needs the accounting department to perform a task, it must go through the CEO. The process is cumbersome and makes terrible use of the CEO's time.

But things can get worse—and in most similarly structured companies, they do. Count on it! Suppose that what IT needs is a piece of hardware to fix a serious computer problem, one so serious that all computers will be down until that part arrives and can be installed, eliminating the problem. As parts must be ordered through the purchasing silo, IT submits a completed purchase order to Purchasing, which then must solicit bids from a minimum of three suppliers. However, Purchasing cannot begin the request-for-price-quotation process until it receives from Accounting authorization to expend funds. Accounting usually only takes a few hours to notify Purchasing that its expenditure request has been authorized, so Purchasing fills its time preparing paperwork and electronic files to dispatch as soon as the okay comes in. The next waiting period begins when the request-for-price-quotations have been sent out and ends when all three bids come back. With bids in, Purchasing selects the low-bid supplier, issues a contract for purchase of the part, and alerts Receiving that delivery should be expected and when. Receiving has its own process to follow before it can accept any delivery: It must complete requisite receiving-silo forms and confirm with Purchasing that the part is an *authorized item,* not merely an *authorized expenditure.*

When all ducks are finally in a row and the selected supplier has delivered, the receiving silo releases the part to IT. Assuming that the broken part was the *only* problem and that IT can bring its computers back up once the new part has been properly installed, they're in business. But think about how much time has elapsed. We can see that each silo performs its tasks in an outstanding manner, but that isn't enough, unfortunately. The outstanding "thoroughness" of each silo does not necessarily work to the benefit of the overall organization. Team goals and performance often conflict with the objectives of organizational silos. Silos protect their turf: If a team solution infringes on one silo's turf, conflict ensues. The best solution is to break down silos.

Putting the "I" into Breaking Down Silos

The first step to breaking down silos is recognizing which silos a team may interact with to accomplish its objective. A team leader can lead team discussion to minimize the potential impact of the silos on team activities.

After all, a team is a horizontal organizational structure, whereas silos are hierarchical, or vertical, organizational structures.

Many organizations flatten their organizational hierarchy in order to minimize the impact of silos. Other organizations, especially ones still heavily dependent on vertical hierarchical structure, may develop silos that impede team effectiveness. A team must determine whether it can succeed within its current organizational structure. If a team believes silos will impede its progress, it must develop strategies to minimize the impact of silos.

Typical Approach to Breaking Down Silos

Many teams ignore how silos may adversely affect their mission. Their philosophy, often unwritten and unspoken, is, *Don't rock the boat.* If a silo prevents completion of an assignment or stands in the way of a solution, a team moves on to other work. In other words, many teams work within their organization's structure and do not waste effort to minimize the impact of organizational silos.

Some teams invite participation from people working externally in organizational units that will be impacted by the team's mission. This approach can be effective, but it frequently fails to address the appropriate organizational level in silos affecting team activities. For example, a team solution involving change in a purchasing department has a chance of succeeding if the team involves the manager of the purchasing department. On the other hand, if the team works with a low-level individual from the purchasing department, that individual may not have the authority or the desire to attempt to change Purchasing's processes.

World-Class Approach to Breaking Down Silos

Teams that want to accomplish their mission must identify silos that may impede their success and then work to minimize the negative impact of these silos. The significant difference between typical and world-class team approaches is recognition of potentially negative silos. Five practices that can help break down or minimize the negative impact of silos are described in the following section.

Five Breaking–Down–Silos Best Team Practices

- *Breaking-Down-Silos Process Best Team Practice 1: Include supportive decision-makers from silos that can affect a team's mission.*

The first staffing challenge a team must address is to identify silos that can negatively affect the team's mission and then find a supporter in each of those silos. Recognizing which silos will affect the mission is normally not difficult. For example, if a team's mission includes enabling the quick acquisition of supplies, the team may determine that the purchasing and accounting departments pose potential negative influence.

A more difficult task is finding an appropriate individual in each potentially prohibitive silo department who both is supportive of the team's mission and possesses authority and decision-making power to assist the team. If a team leader or another team member is familiar with one of these silo departments, he or she can probably suggest appropriate individuals. If no one on the team has specific knowledge of staff working in these silos, the team leader may need to enlist the help of someone outside the team. For example, if the purchasing department is a potentially prohibitive silo, team members should talk to someone with experience requesting purchases through the purchasing department to identify a supporter with appropriate authority.

- *Breaking-Down-Silos Process Best Team Practice 2: Diagram how each department or silo really works.*

It would be easy to mistake a pitcher for the pitch-selection decision-maker on a baseball team. In fact, a catcher typically determines the pitch. In other instances, the first- or third-base coach calls the pitch. Without investigating how an organization really works, a team may not enlist the appropriate person in a silo and may lose the opportunity to break down a silo's opposition.

Within any organizational unit are two hierarchies, at a minimum. One is the formal structure that is outlined by job titles and models of information and workflow. The second reflects how work is really accomplished—frequently in a convoluted and patched-together fashion.

When a team works with a silo department, it may at first be inclined to believe the department functions according to its formal organization. Team members must learn, however, to identify a silo's actual working structure. For example, an organizational unit typically includes multiple subject-matter experts. If a decision needs to be made within one area of expertise, a team should consult the appropriate subject-matter expert. In the silo's formal hierarchy, this subject-matter expert may be three levels down the official ladder but may actually function at the top level for certain types of decisions. If the team is unaware of how the organizational unit really works, it may go to the wrong individual for a decision and approval.

A silo department may perform, say, five different activities but only one of those might negatively affect a team's mission. When diagramming how a silo really works, a team need only concern itself with that one relevant activity. Diagrams should identify key decision-makers and show the relationships between decision-makers and other high-level individuals in the silo.

- *Breaking-Down-Silos Process Best Team Practice 3: Assess pushing the limits of a team's authority.*

Many businesses roughly outline each department's authority and responsibilities. These guidelines rightly include gray areas, leaving room for fluctuation depending on particular environments and projects. Back when I was a department supervisor, one of my staff members asked to be sent to a training course he deemed crucial to completion of a job assignment. I knew I did not have authority to approve travel and expenses, but my department head, who could approve travel and tuition, was on vacation and would not return in time to make the decision. I signed the requisition, the accounting department advanced funds, and off went my happy staff member to class.

When my department head returned, I told her what had taken place, and she confirmed that I'd made the correct decision. Amazingly, we didn't even discuss the fact that I had exceeded what in later years I came to call my *situational* authority. From the experience, I realized that many people possess situational authority but fail to use it, staying within the boundaries of a formal job description.

For most teams, authority and responsibilities are not particularly well defined. Ambiguity functions like speed limits in districts that recommend "reasonable and prudent" speed instead of a miles-per-hour limit—that is, not well at all! Teams should push such authority as much as needed so that team members can accomplish their mission.

One of my early computer-science heroes was actually a heroine: Grace Hopper. A naval officer of military mind, Hopper held the view that it is easier to obtain forgiveness for acting correctly without authority than it is to get permission for the action in advance. (According to programming lore, she also coined the term "bug" for a software defect—but I digress.) If teams push the limits of their authority and do what's best for business, they usually will be forgiven. However, Hopper also went on to explain two conditions that must exist if someone intends to exceed what might be considered his or her limits of authority. The first condition is that whatever is done must be done in the employer's best interest; the second is that no one blatantly override authority, pushing limits only within gray areas that are subject to interpretation.

Most supervisors would rather grant forgiveness than permission. If a supervisor is not asked for permission, he or she may not be held accountable (although it is my view that supervisors are responsible for whatever actions their people take, regardless of whether supervisory permission has been granted). The message supervisors convey when it appears that they would rather give forgiveness than permission is that they are willing to let the team exceed its authority in the interest of getting the job done. If the team succeeds, the supervisor will look as good as the team. If the team fails, the supervisor may stoop to stating that the team exceeded authority without permission.

- *Breaking-Down-Silos Process Best Team Practice 4: Collect and measure data to leverage for mission support.*

The *cost of quality* can be stated as the difference between the cost of building a product or service right the first time and the actual cost when multiple re-builds and re-do's must be performed until the product or service is viable. The time it takes to find defects and to rebuild correctly working software is a cost of quality, calculated in terms of salaries paid and revenues lost or postponed because of late delivery.

When a team performs cost analysis prior to beginning working with a specific silo, it should be on the watch for departmental practices that are costly but without merit in the context of the planned project. When presenting statistical proof of the cost of a silo's specific, poor performance, for example, a team needs to be careful to make its point tactfully without causing embarrassment to that silo. Embarrassing statistics can be uncovered and documented in such a way as to assure that a silo's resistance to working with the team and cooperating with its mission will not increase.

- *Breaking-Down-Silos Process Best Team Practice 5: Define benefits for stakeholder silos.*

When people face a new or additional assignment, they frequently wonder, "What's in it for me?" If a team can thoroughly define benefits of working toward the team mission to a silo department, it can craft a more potentially successful plan for all parties.

Whenever a proposal requires someone to lose while another wins, there is going to be opposition to that proposal. However, if a team can convert a silo's "lose" situation into a "win" situation, it probably can get its recommendation implemented. For example, if an organization allows departmental units to drive through emergency requisitions, bypassing, say, the purchasing department, the purchasing department appears to lose some authority within the organization. However, if a team credits Purchasing for identifying a problem and developing a solution, Purchasing looks like it has done something very beneficial. This strategy, of course, reduces the credit the team itself might receive for whatever it has proposed, but it garners cooperation, permitting the team to better accomplish its mission.

Impediments to the Breaking–Down–Silos Challenge

When a silo resists or opposes a team's mission, it may believe it must do so to protect its turf, to defend practices tied in to long-standing process, or to conform with what it believes is best for the business as a whole. Just as teams have missions, so, too, do silos have missions. If a team's recommendations threaten to change or lessen a silo's mission, the silo is likely to object. The mentality expressed as "we've always done it this way and our plan is to continue to do it this way" protects silo personnel against negative effects of change, including possible reductions in staff, budget, authority, and responsibility.

People can be fiercely loyal to long-standing processes. A silo that over decades has developed and continually improved a process until achieving what it regards as an outstanding level of performance is not likely to welcome new ways. Although it is possible that the silo is doing the *wrong* thing very efficiently, getting it to change can be exceptionally difficult. A team will need tact and skill to convert its recommendations into a change in silo process. Several activities might need to occur, including writing changes into the process or creating a completely new process, for example. To effect change, team members may need to consider deleting tasks from the existing process, convincing individuals in the silo organization that the change is positive and to their benefit, providing required training and support, and so on.

A team at odds with a silo as to what is best for the business has its work cut out for it. After years of working in a certain way without criticism, a silo can become convinced that its activity contributes to the betterment of the business—regardless of reality. Any change could be viewed as conflicting with what's best for the organization. A team must sell its change, presenting it in terms of benefit to the silo as well as to the organization.

Strategies to Overcome the Breaking-Down-Silos Challenge

Teams can work toward breaking down resistance from a silo by identifying and engaging a team-mission champion. The team itself may not be able to work effectively with a silo to obtain approval for a change to the silo's processes; however, enlisting a champion who commands the respect of a silo's management can minimize negative impact on the mission.

Another way a team may be able to minimize negative impact is by aligning its mission with the silo's mission. The team may need to adapt or modify its mission so that it is consistent with all or part of the silo's mission. If, for example, a purchasing department's mission includes a phrase such as "meeting the needs of the departments of the organization," an IT team can then incorporate that phrase and attitude into its mission.

Breaking–Down–Silos Plan of Action

A simple method teams can use to help themselves identify potential negative impact is to define their team mission in multiple ways. One way might be to select among three variations of a team-mission statement, citing, for example, the best mission, a good mission, and an achievable mission. If a team faces insurmountable obstacles to its "best mission," it can hope to orchestrate transition through a back-up plan—that is, by focusing, say, on an "achievable mission." If a team's recommendation would challenge a silo's long-standing process, it must convince individuals in the silo that the change benefits them, that they will receive necessary training and support, and so on.

10

Challenge 8:
Avoiding Groupthink

A song in the musical *South Pacific* tells us that when our behavior and attitudes are marked by a hatred, it is because "people have been carefully taught." For example, a sports team may harbor an inherited bitterness toward its primary rival, but there is real danger in such preprogrammed behavior. That danger is that the team may focus on developing plays and strategies to beat the one rival, but will find itself ineffective against many of the other teams it will play during a season. Conformity to group values and the practice of reverting to a common mentality without thinking through its consequences and implications is called "groupthink."

Groupthink prevails in many business teams. The inclination of team members to agree with each other and to swiftly, unanimously, "get things done" can actually impede the success of their mission. For example, a purchasing team that assumes that a specific software package can only be acquired from one manufacturer could exclude consideration of other manufacturers, an assumption that may prevent the team from meeting its exit criteria.

Groupthink is particularly harmful because it is self-perpetuating. People conform to a certain way of thinking without realizing their indoctrination. For example, a software development team might have tried using a new programming language for a project that ultimately failed. Members of the organization tell each other it failed because the programming language is inferior; they don't bother to investigate whether the project failed due to an ineffective implementation plan or some other cause.

Everyone on a team needs both to understand that groupthink can exist and to recognize when it taints decisions. Recognizing that groupthink exists does involve more than just paying lip service to the idea. If a member of the team does not recognize the function and potential dangers of groupthink, he or she may believe rational consensus has been reached when in fact the team has fallen victim to groupthink. To avoid this danger, team members may challenge decisions that may have resulted from groupthink. If consensus occurs quickly, for example, people can further test both the decision made and each team member's role in reaching consensus. Members can question whether other rational alternatives should be considered and whether people thoroughly vetted their own commitment to achieving the best solution.

Putting the "I" into Avoiding Groupthink

Some years ago, I was discussing team strategies with a colleague from India and mentioned the concept of buy-in. My colleague looked puzzled and said that although he'd heard the term, he really didn't know what it meant. I explained that when someone wants support for changing an existing element or adding a new feature, he or she presents what is hoped to be a compelling benefits summary to each person or group that is likely to be affected. With "buy-in," the modification is more likely to be approved and to succeed in its mission. My colleague replied that, in India, what the boss wants is what the workers want—that is, everyone obeys the boss.

Such mass acceptance of someone else's declaration or action signifies a type of mob psychology that can affect matters in both positive and negative ways. One or two people can influence a large group of people to think or behave a certain way. This is one possible reason why presumably otherwise civilized soccer fans turn into raging mobs capable of exacting great damage to property and limb when excited by a play.

Many teams expend a lot of effort trying to garner buy-in for their recommendations from team members and other involved parties. Groupthink can play a positive role in the context of buy-in. If one or two influential individuals on a team push a particular concept, others in the group tend to go along with what those few want, even though they personally may not fully agree with the recommendation. This form of consensus, however, is not a genuine buy-in to the concept, because team members merely go along with the recommendation rather than truly endorsing it.

A danger of groupthink is that it both influences people to believe that the group is correct and quashes independent thinking. What transpires is similar to what happens when a person performs some task and then checks his or her own work for accuracy. A letter writer is not likely to be the best person to proofread and find errors in the letter just written, perhaps because his or her mind is so focused on the process that it's difficult to see defects in the result.

When wielded positively, groupthink puts the "I" in team-work because it raises the level of each individual's contribution to team activities. Individuals do not become subsumed by the group, but rather are major contributors to it. When we discourage positive groupthink, we open the door to the individual's dissension.

Typical Approach to Avoiding Groupthink

Many teams view groupthink as little more than forming consensus about an idea, believing that when a group reaches consensus it has reached the best solution. Typically, teams tacitly encourage groupthink. This does not mean that such teams say, "Let's go think like a group." It means that teams try to encourage consensus. Individuals who interfere with groupthink are some-times viewed negatively—even when they raise legitimate concerns. People who are reluctant to follow the herd can end up feeling like outsiders. If a dissenter fears losing support, whether personal or professional, he or she may stop suggesting ideas and will sign on with the group, keeping fundamental disagreement under wraps. This is not a healthy environment for the dissenter or for the consenters.

World–Class Approach to Avoiding Groupthink

To assess both positive and negative aspects of groupthink, teams must train themselves to recognize when groupthink is in play. During their organizational project-planning stage, teams should discuss both the pros and the cons of groupthink. One advantage, for example, might be that when groupthink builds consensus and limits second-guessing, the team can properly focus its effort. One disadvantage could be that groupthink may intimidate people into withholding valuable input during the decision-making process.

Just how this works is easy to see in the sports world. Football teams need to be ruled by a kind of groupthink when the coach calls a play because players are not to make decisions contrary to what is mandated by the coach. However, coaches do not want groupthink to prevail among assistant coaches; instead, they want recommendations for lineups and substitutions, play-call assessments, and whatever other advice assistant coaches can offer to help the team win. When discussion ends, however, the coach decides the next play.

Practices teams can implement in order to avoid the negative implications of groupthink include defining a team decision-making process, inviting an adversary to join the team, allowing team members to vote by secret ballot, developing an anti-groupthink checklist, and evaluating team effectiveness at predetermined checkpoints throughout a project. These five practices are discussed in the sections that follow.

Five Groupthink–Avoidance Best Team Practices

- *Avoiding-Groupthink Process Best Team Practice 1: Define a process and method for team decision-making.*

The United States Supreme Court is a high-level illustration of groupthink at its best. The Court has nine justices; a simple majority of five decides the opinion of the Court. However, any justice who refrains from delivering a decision or who disagrees with the majority decision may include with the Court's opinion a commentary detailing his or her position.

A team might decide to require all members' concurrence to make a recommendation to management, or that a simple majority is adequate. A team may decide it will only make one recommendation, or that it will supply a preferred recommendation accompanied by alternatives. Teams should determine whether what appears to be a unanimous decision is indeed unanimous.

Dissenting individuals who feel coerced to consent may contribute to subsequent project failure if their opposition is not intelligently addressed.

- *Avoiding-Groupthink Process Best Team Practice 2: Invite support for the team's objective from possible adversarial outsiders.*

If a team includes someone who does not support its mission, that person will most likely challenge the team's approach. For example, if an IT department is considering hiring independent testers and someone within the IT department does not support independent testing, that person would be a good addition to the team. If the team can win over that adversary to approve independent testing, it gains valuable experience needed, perhaps, to win over other adversaries within the organization. An opposing viewpoint can also help teams assess the effects of groupthink. For example, if that adversary presented valid reasons against independent testing, some team members who would have gone along with whatever solution the majority formed may change their minds because they better understand an alternative solution.

- *Avoiding-Groupthink Process Best Team Practice 3: Allow team members to vote secretly on recommended team actions.*

Many teams do not vote on the content of or whether to present a recommendation because no opposition or dissension is made public. A team leader may see no support for a plan or action when he or she asks for a show of hands, but secretly cast ballots may reveal a majority in favor.

Movies, theatrical productions, television shows, and books by the thousands depict trial juries deliberating verdicts (a process known to most everyone over the age of two). Because juries vote secretly, individual jurors can vote their conscience, and are not *as subject to peer pressure* as they would be if publicly declaring a decision. Jurors may debate a particular verdict for hours, days, weeks, and even months, but until all members of the jury concur, there is no verdict. Every juror must be certain, beyond reasonable doubt, that the verdict is correct. The judicial process allows individuals to delay a decision and discussion to continue.

For teams, the practice of casting a secret ballot for or against something is simple: Team members mark their ballots and place them in a box. Someone designated to collect ballots counts the votes for and against a proposal and announces the result. If team members agree that only a simple majority is needed, one vote can decide a matter. However, if team members rule for a unanimous vote and one is not reached, discussion continues. It's just that simple.

- *Avoiding-Groupthink Process Best Team Practice 4: Develop an anti-groupthink checklist.*

An anti-groupthink checklist can be drawn up from a list of questions team members ask themselves before arriving at a recommendation. Important topics to cover follow:

1. What alternative recommendations, if any, should we consider?
2. Has this recommendation been successfully tried before? If ineffective, why?
3. Is management likely to support this recommendation? If not, why?
4. Are our coworkers, customers, and users likely to support this recommendation? If not, why?
5. Does this recommendation include sufficient detail so that people implementing it can understand it?
6. Are there sufficient resources available to implement this recommendation?

When a team develops a recommendation, it should discuss each anti-groupthink checklist question to determine whether the recommendation is a product of groupthink. This approach helps assure that adequate discussion and analysis shape a recommendation and that the recommendation, therefore, has a higher probability of being implemented successfully.

- *Avoiding-Groupthink Process Best Team Practice 5: Invite individuals to evaluate team effectiveness at periodic checkpoints.*

Some things are easy. It is easy, for example, for a team's activities and discussions to wander off-track. It is easy for one or two members of a team to dominate discussion. It is easy for a team leader to impose, whether intentionally or not, his or her decisions on a team. It is *not* so easy to improve a team's recommendation-development method if people evaluate it only after the fact.

In order to evaluate effectiveness at periodic checkpoints, a team must perform self-analysis. If, for example, a team expects to complete a mission in three days, it should perform a self-analysis, say, at the end of each of the first and second days. Each member of the team should perform a self-analysis, providing written answers to questions such as the following:

1. Is any team member dominating our discussion?
2. Has our team leader imposed decisions or mandated direction without first listening to and considering our input?
3. Are we effectively using the time available for team activities?
4. Are we each allowing other team members adequate time to express their opinions?
5. Have we assessed the potential impact of our recommendation—for ourselves and other departments?

At each checkpoint, team members should complete the self-analysis questionnaire and return it anonymously to someone designated to tally responses. Once the team considers the responses, team members should gather as a group to discuss them. If several responses share a concern, say, that one person dominates discussion, the entire team should address the issue. The self-analysis should never serve as evidence for reprimand or as a performance evaluation, and should never be conducted in such a way as to make it obvious who, for instance, dominates discussion. Resolution should be owned by all on the team.

Impediments to the Groupthink–Avoidance Challenge

Two problems organizations face trying to understand the effects of groupthink relate to team camaraderie and schedule. In terms of the first, efforts to avoid groupthink can minimize team camaraderie. When teams appear to be cohesive, team spirit rises. However, if a process allows adversaries to continually disrupt what appears to be an otherwise intact, fully functional group, camaraderie may decrease and the team's overall effectiveness may decrease. By carefully planning how to encourage individuals to express dissenting opinions—even to the extent that this delays decisions—a team can build cohesion as it refines its mission.

Efforts to avoid groupthink may extend the time a team needs to arrive at a consensus conclusion. If teams encourage individuals to present dissenting opinions, team members will need time to consider the merit of these opinions. Even if an opinion itself is unjustified or impractical, teams may benefit from discussing related pros and cons. While this activity may not necessarily lead directly to a recommendation, the habit of fruitful discussion can help participants avoid poor recommendations.

Strategies to Overcome the Groupthink–Avoidance Challenge

A strategy to overcome the groupthink challenge must strengthen team leadership characteristics and structure team activities to incorporate sufficient time to accomplish essential tasks. Team leaders must be able to *lead*. This competency (initially discussed in Chapter 3) remains vital to the success of a team as it strives to accomplish its mission. If avoiding groupthink reduces team camaraderie or unnecessarily extends the time a team takes to do assignments, the leader must step in to ensure that the team acts in the most effective and efficient manner. For example, if someone on the team keeps raising the same objection to a potential recommendation, the team leader may decide to terminate discussion, saying, "We've already discussed this and determined it is not valid in our context." If the team leader is an effective leader, he or she can maintain camaraderie while keeping the team on track.

Another groupthink challenge to overcome is how to allocate enough time to different team activities. For example, meetings may need to be restricted to one hour. The team leader is responsible for ensuring that a team continues to effectively complete its work, perhaps by cutting off or delaying discussion, or by scheduling a future meeting with individual team members to maximize the value of the current hour.

Groupthink–Avoidance Plan of Action

Avoiding groupthink is primarily the team leaders' responsibility. Team leaders need to recognize the potential pitfalls and opportunities associated with groupthink and devise a plan consisting of at least the following three actions: They must be prepared to discuss the concept of groupthink when organizing potential team members for a project; they must be able to recognize when groupthink may have occurred; and they must be able to independently assess proposed team recommendations. Recognizing when consensus appears to occur too quickly can be a daunting task, but a team leader needs to raise questions that force team members to address negative aspects of automaton consensus. Team leaders also must be able to review team recommendations with key people in departments affected by a proposed change. They must carefully evaluate recommendations, present them logically, and verify that the organization can implement them.

11

Challenge 9: Assuring That Team Efforts Are Successful

One of the biggest mistakes that individuals, teams, and organizations make in business is starting a project but never finishing it. Among the many causes of unfinished projects are a lack of planning, resources, competency, follow-through, and the desire to succeed.

My grandfather was a successful real-estate developer. He kept motivational statements like the following posted on his walls:

- Thought is the inspiration of action, but the *thing done* is what counts.
- The world is full of starters but few finishers.
- All worthwhile achievements are the result of an idea, a start, and a strong finish.
- People think all man needs is initiative, but action must be sustained to be effective.
- The cause of most failure is lack of action, the predominant error in every walk of life.
- Few brilliant ideas ever see the light of day, represented as they chiefly are by much talk and little action.
- Thomas Edison devoted twenty-two hours a day to putting his ideas into action.
- Think of a sale, pitch the sale—don't quit until the sale is closed.
- The course of least resistance is the road to the scrap heap.
- It takes determination and stamina to maintain action.
- There is no greater ending than *it is done.*

To increase my chances of finishing a slew of projects that had me in knots some years ago, I applied two organizational skunk-works theories. One, the double-cut theory, I used to secure adequate resources to complete a project. By doubling the budget I thought I would need to do a project correctly, I had sufficient funding even after management, in its infinite wisdom, cut my budget in half, which inevitably it did.

The second skunk-works theory that I applied as a project leader trying to lock in sufficient resources to assure project success is the rat-hole theory. Considerably more challenging than the double-cut theory, the rat-hole theory instructs recalculation of the return on investment at the point at which a project's budget is used up, disappearing, as it were, down a rat hole. This is the point at which the project potentially will exceed its budget. To see how this works, suppose that a project budgeted at five-hundred-thousand dollars promises to yield benefits of one million dollars— a 100-percent return on investment. But now suppose that as the project nears completion, it runs out of money and requires an additional hundred-thousand dollars to complete. Recalculating the ROI solely on the additional hundred-thousand dollars, the million dollars becomes a return on investment of 1,000 percent. Pretty nice! What started out as a 100-percent return on investment can be posited as a 1,000-percent return.

Putting the "I" into Assuring Team Success

Every team member must take personal responsibility for project success, internalizing the belief, "If it's going to be, it's up to me." The "me" in the saying must take the lead, refusing to say no to shouldering responsibility and being willing to put in the time and effort required for the project's success. A project's best chance at success depends, in fact, on putting the "I"—the "me"—back in the team.

Typical Approach to Assuring Team Success

Inner suspicions about teamwork such as the following—if left unchecked—actually can cause projects to fail:

- You won't do anything wrong if you don't do anything at all.
- Never volunteer.
- Do what you're told to do, not what you know you should do.
- Act busy all the time and complain that you're over-worked.

Unfortunately, the typical approach to team success ignores the necessity of the success of individual team members. Put another way, the prevailing attitude is that members of a team have no individual responsibility for failure; it is the fault of the entire team.

Many teams completely lack responsibility for their recommendations. In a previous example, we discussed a team deciding whether or not to form an independent test team within the IT department. The team might recommend the use of independent testing and then dissolve. Without the continuous support and investment of those recommending a change, its implementation may fail.

Many team members believe they are assigned to a team to accomplish specific tasks (completed individually or with other team members). However, they limit their responsibility to the completion of those tasks: They assume no responsibility for how individual tasks integrate as a solution, how a solution is rolled out, or whether a solution is successful.

World–Class Approach to Assuring Team Success

No one can *guarantee* success. However, the probability of success can increase greatly with good leadership that motivates team members to succeed. If team leaders have succeeded in the past, knowledge of that success helps motivate individuals joining a team: They can believe that history of success will continue for their team.

Take the New York Yankees, for example, a Major League baseball team that for many years seemed to have an aura of invincibility. Those who study the sport maintain that a baseball player who puts on a Yankees' uniform actually hits and fields better than when wearing another team's uniform. Die-hard fans of the New

York Mets, the Boston Red Sox, the Colorado Rockies, and of probably most every other team in Major League baseball see things differently but, if true, one reason a player of average talent may play better in a Yankees' uniform is that the Yankees, as a team, *expect* to win. The confidence and cockiness—let's not call it arrogance—stirs non-Yankees' fans to snipe, "I root for my home team and any team that beats the New York Yankees."

With the Yankees, winning is a tradition, a religion, *and a business*—their desire to win and their confidence that they can win are attributes IT project teammates would be wise to emulate. For example, if a team leader engenders the attitude that his or her team is going to make a difference, people start to believe it will make a difference. Bolstering that attitude with proper planning, adequate resources, supplemental training, and hands-on command of the best practices discussed in this book can go far toward ensuring team success.

To help assure success, teams can execute the following best practices, which affect how a team approaches problems, makes recommendations, and monitors performance in the context of what is in the best interest of the organization.

Five Assuring–Team–Success Best Team Practices

* *Assuring-Team-Success Process Best Team Practice 1: Propose feasible recommendations and achievable projects.*

Before teams offer recommendations or commence implementing change, they must assess whether the solutions are achievable, and if so, with success at what level—high, moderate, low, or, hopefully never, zero. Characteristics of an achievable solution include its consistency with the goals and objectives of the organization, adequate resources and time, staff competency, and assurance that the solution will not negatively affect other projects. A project team can consider a solution's suitability by answering questions such as the following:

* Does the solution align with organizational objectives and goals?
* Does it warrant priority of implementation?

- Will the organization commit staff and resources, as needed, to implement it?
- Do staff members assigned to implement the solution unequivocally support the project?

- *Assuring-Team-Success Process Best Team Practice 2: Align stakeholders with the team's objective.*

Team leaders must garner support from all stakeholders to increase the probability of a project's success. Their first step is to identify project stakeholders having a vested interest in the project's success. Stakeholders may well include allies as well as individuals who are yet to be won over to the merits of the project. Among stakeholders may be people who want to lead the project, who want to help the project succeed, who have no interest in whether the project succeeds or fails, and even some who actively want the project to fail.

Team members may ask stakeholders which category best describes their interest, but their answers cannot be relied upon. The team itself must determine whether it can convert to a supporter a stakeholder who, say, wants the project to fail. If a team cannot persuade people who want a project to fail to change their position, it must determine whether to proceed or whether it should propose an alternative version of the project.

- *Assuring-Team-Success Process Best Team Practice 3: Engage appropriate levels of management as active contributors to project success.*

Workers tend to emulate examples set for them by management; they do not as readily carry out what management says to do if it differs from what management does. For example, management may give lip service to tight security, but if it does not follow through by punishing individuals who jeopardize security, say, by displaying their password on a sticky note on their computer terminal, the breach will magnify.

A management strategy that some humorously call Management By Walking Around can be used to gauge management's involvement in each project's success. I personally witnessed the opposite of this strategy when I decades ago consulted at a multinational corporation with an exceptionally large staff. I asked a senior VP where a certain cadre of key staff members was located, and was answered by silence and a blank stare. While this response may not be typical, most managers do not really know the details of how their staff completes work assignments.

A team's success in vetting a solution, then, depends on not only the commitment of workers implementing it but also on the attitude of managers governing follow-through. Managers may increase effective involvement in ways such as the following:

- They may attend team meetings.
- They may review team recommendations before approving them and suggest ways to improve the chance for success.
- They may solicit discussion of interim goals and work status as agenda items at staff meetings.
- They may track resources and monitor budget items to help the team control challenges.

- *Assuring-Team-Success Process Best Team Practice 4: Always do what is best for the organization itself.*

Too frequently, team members are so involved in completing individual assignments that they do not adequately consider the overall benefit their work brings to their organization. For example, an IT department may recommend acquisition of the latest computer technology without considering overall implications of cost versus benefit to their organization. New technology may be outstanding, but the technology may not provide sufficient benefits to justify the cost or the effort staff will need to expend to learn to use it.

Doing what is best for business does not always equate to executing the most popular recommendation. Many organizations outsource various activities in order to benefit in areas of cost or quality. A decision to outsource call-centers, often located abroad, may not be popular within the organization but may be an intelligent business decision. Doing what is best for business includes evaluating human factors in business decisions. Persuading stakeholders remains essential. If, for instance, worker morale and customer satisfaction would plummet due to outsourcing a call-center, the financial benefits are not likely to offset taking that action.

- *Assuring-Team-Success Process Best Team Practice 5: Build team commitment to the success of its recommendations.*

I many times have asked people whether they are willing to bet their job on a recommendation's success. Like many other bosses, when I hear people share recommendations with me, I'm inclined to discount the idea until I know how committed the person is to making that idea successful. I have learned over and over that people make recommendations easily, but many are reluctant to personally commit to making those recommendations succeed.

If I reject someone's recommendation and he or she reworks it and proposes it again, I have much more confidence that the person is committed to the success of the recommendation. Only after witnessing this type of commitment will I approve a recommendation. I want people to work on projects that they feel compelled to complete.

Impediments to the Assuring-Team-Success Challenge

Teams face a multitude of obstacles when striving for success. One difficulty comes in connection with their inability to accept responsibility for success; another is their failure to ensure that their solutions and recommendations are practical and feasible; yet another comes from management if it is not committed to project success.

Many teams operate under the philosophy that management appoints them to perform a specific task. The task "belongs" to management. When team members complete an assignment or offer management a recommendation, they believe their work is done. For example, if management assigned Task X to a team, it would complete Task X and never think about it again. Even if during the completion of Task X a team suspects it is not in the organization's best interest or knows that changing focus or scope would improve the quality of its work, team members remain silent because these decisions are not viewed as their responsibility.

An obstacle to be reckoned with is that many teams do not care whether their assignment is, for them, impossible to perform or poorly designed. Teams that take sufficient time to determine the doability of a project might not have recommended it, or might have recommended that it be achieved in a different fashion. Studies we conducted at the Quality Assurance Institute show that the number-one success criterion reported by surveyed users of software is that the software meet their requirements. A disconnect occurs when poorly defined or incompatible requirements infiltrate design plans.

But arguably the greatest impediment occurs when management has not committed to the success of a project. Not infrequently, management distances itself from a project, possibly because one level of management may pressure underlings to undertake a project that the underlings believe will not succeed. Lower-level management assigns a team that forms a recommendation, but neither the team nor those who formed the recommendation commit to its success. Such politicking does not bode well for the success of the project.

Strategies to Overcome the Team–Success Challenge

If I wanted to build a house but knew it could not be completed within the constraints of my budget, I wouldn't sign a document authorizing the project. It is not difficult for most people to know whether a project can attain successful completion. Three strategies that can help team members determine when to stop or rework a project are oriented toward assuring team success.

First, if a team will not accept responsibility for a project's success, the team leader may stop or rework the project. Managers should ask team members whether they are willing to bet their jobs on a project's success. If they are not, team leaders can elect to reject or rework the project until team members are confident and stake responsibility in its success.

Second, a project that is not doable should not be approved. Potential challenges or roadblocks that might cause a project to fail should be examined and evaluated. If, for instance, lack of competency or lack of resources threatens a project's success, either obtain needed training or resources or abandon or postpone the project.

Third, team success depends on having management's commitment to its success. Therefore, managers must ask themselves how much of their time, effort, and reputation they are willing to invest in assuring success. Managers must understand what chance the project has for success. If the answer is, "minimal," the project should not be undertaken or, if undertaken, at the very least it should be reworked.

Assuring–Team–Success Plan of Action

As a team leader, I never wanted to be associated with a project with a high probability of failure. Who would? My years in the software industry have taught me that many project leaders do start projects with little chance of success and then leave the project, "promoted" before their solution is implemented. I've also met many IT managers who never worked on a project through implementation.

By determining the probability of a project's success *before* undertaking it, team leaders increase the likelihood of the team's success. Feasibility, management support, and adequate resources significantly affect a project's chances. Potential team members should only sign on for projects that meet entrance criteria.

In addition, team members who sign a written commitment to project success usually will be more committed to assuring project success. Factors such as a willingness to work extra hours, a commitment to assuring assistance so that other team members won't fail, and a dedication to working with customers all affect success.

12

Challenge 10: Rewarding Individual Team Members

When my children were in elementary school, they would get a star or some form of recognition for a well-executed assignment. Some teachers gave out points for good behavior and rewarded students who accumulated a certain number of points. The philosophy behind this reward system is the same one I used as a boy teaching my dogs tricks, giving praise or a treat when the behavior was what I was looking for.

Rewards recognize achievement but they also motivate, providing a reason to continue for excellence (in the case of the recognized individual) and to strive to excel (in the hearts and minds of onlookers). Motivational rewards come in many sizes and flavors. For example, Little League baseball teammates may be treated to pizza and ice-cream sodas after they win a game. Players on the NFL team that wins the Super Bowl each receive a special ring to commemorate their victory. High-school athletes who complete a season of a particular sport may get a letter sweater or a jacket with the school emblem on it. Parents of honor students may get stickers to affix to the bumpers of their cars that boast, "My child is an Honor Student at the ABC School."

Most dogs are happy with treats or praise but people are harder to please because different people like different types of rewards. Some people see working flex-hours as a reward, some want recognition in front of their peers, some enjoy seeing their photograph in the company newsletter, others want money. The bottom line is, team members who are effective in carrying out their team responsibilities should be recognized. Rewards do work in training dogs; rewards may work in getting individual team members to put extra effort and time into performing their tasks.

Putting the "I" into Rewarding Individual Team Members

Many winning sports teams are guided by the philosophy that no individual team member wins a game, and no individual team member loses a game. Winning and losing are team activities. Winning requires, however, that each team member fulfill individual responsibilities in an effective and efficient manner.

Employees should challenge themselves to correlate what they do on a day-to-day basis with the success of their department and organization. Labor organizers know all too well that when a company for which their union members work is losing money, it is unlikely to reward its workers, despite their documented success. Understanding the relationship between performance and rewards requires an open mind. One way to effectively utilize rewards to motivate teamwork is to author an agreement to be signed both by those who give rewards and by those who do the work, stating exactly how rewards are earned and distributed.

Typical Approach to Rewarding Individual Team Members

Organizations typically reward individuals based on results of their regular work assignments but rarely give recognition for what they do as part of a team. Even worse, team members may suffer *because of teamwork,* receiving little or no recognition for the excellent regular work they've personally accomplished. Another way team members may suffer because of teamwork is that team activities take time away from regular work.

If teamwork is rewarded, most often the team is recognized but individuals are not. Without even minimal recognition, people may become demoralized. However, rewarding individuals can be a sensitive matter. If one team member thinks he or she has made a major contribution but is rewarded in a manner identical to another team member who is perceived as having made no contribution, the contributing team member could consider the organization to be unfair. But the damage goes beyond the confines of the team. Individuals on other existing teams who learn of the inequity may not be motivated to work their hardest.

World–Class Approach to Rewarding Individual Team Members

Sports teams offer an array of rewards. Consider these common scenarios:

- After a victory, the football coach gives a game ball to the day's most-valuable player.
- After a baseball player hits a home run, teammates from the dugout run out to congratulate him as he crosses home plate.
- After a golfer in a foursome hits a long fairway drive or sinks a tricky putt, the other players ooze praise, saying, *"Great* shot."
- After a basketball player sinks a foul shot, teammates exuberantly exchange high-fives and body-pats.

When a coach or a teammate pats a player on the back after a good play, he or she sends a message that the player is appreciated. Why do so few business teams and organizations exhibit the same behavior? When one team member sitting at a conference table makes a great suggestion, why don't the other team members give that individual high-fives? Why doesn't the team leader say, *"Great* idea"? Why doesn't the senior manager pop in and thank the person for the suggestion? The answer in most instances is not that management, the team leader, and the team members just don't care; they just don't understand the value of such appreciation. They may never have experienced the support typical in team sports, and they may never have really been given significant appreciation themselves.

World-class business teams should reward individual team members, both periodically throughout team activities as well as at the end of a project. Periodic rewards motivate individuals to break large, complex, or intimidating assignments into doable chunks. For teams to be most effective, the rewards system needs to change. Five best team practices that can be used to reward individual team members are described in the paragraphs that follow.

Five Individual–Team–Member–Rewards Best Team Practices

- *Rewarding-Individual-Team-Members Process Best Team Practice 1: Customize rewards to best thank and motivate each individual.*

Some years ago when a colleague and I were discussing ways to motivate and reward individuals, she surprised me by saying that no single reward will satisfy all individuals. She gave the example of an employee being invited out for dinner by the boss. I quickly saw her point: Such an invitation may exhilarate one individual but seriously infringe on another's personal time. My colleague went on to describe the different ways she rewards individuals, favoring periodic rewards as opposed to annual performance appraisals, pay raises, and promotions.

The discussion led us to conclude that until an organization discovers what motivates someone, it cannot develop an appropriate reward mechanism. The way to find out what motivates specific individuals is to ask them—and to gauge their response to earned rewards.

This best practice requires team leaders to ask individual team members privately what types of rewards they feel appropriately compensate for significant contribution to team activities. If a team leader cannot fulfill team members' requests, he or she needs to attempt to identify a desirable reward the organization can provide.

- *Rewarding-Individual-Team-Members Process Best Team Practice 2: Reward in public, criticize in private.*

Most people appreciate being given some form of recognition for outstanding work. An exceptionally good waiter or waitress certainly will appreciate your generous tip but may benefit equally if you mention the outstanding service to his or her manager or the restaurant's owner. Similarly, team members who have done a great job for me never seem to tire of my telling their supervisor about their outstanding performance.

Another "public" reward that I usually have found to be appreciated is to recognize individuals in the company of their family or friends. Inviting an individual's spouse or companion to attend an awards dinner honoring the person or giving the person a gift certificate for dinner for two at a restaurant or box seats at a sporting event are generally viewed as rewards worth receiving. In addition, taking the time to write a personal letter thanking the individual for an outstanding contribution scores high on the recognition charts.

When, on the other hand, a team member performs poorly or fails to follow proscribed procedures, it is appropriate to offer criticism in the form of objective analysis and assessment, conveyed in private. Criticizing a person in front of peers exacts an emotional—and professional—cost. Doing so can negate any positive recognition of an individual's work. The reason for sharing criticism should be to help individuals improve, not to punish them.

- *Rewarding-Individual-Team-Members Process Best Team Practice 3: Identify and reward innovation.*

Organizations must continually develop new approaches if they are to become or to remain competitive. Continuous process improvement can generate small gains in productivity and quality, but innovation can lead to significant breakthroughs, improving productivity and quality. Thomas Edison reportedly quipped that he learned more than a hundred ways *not* to make an electric light bulb. If Edison had not still desired to invent a workable electric light bulb after more than one-hundred failed attempts, he probably never would have succeeded. Intermittent failure, as a learning-and-development tool, is an important part of innovation.

- *Rewarding-Individual-Team-Members Process Best Team Practice 4: Enlist team members' support for rewarding individuals.*

One top Fortune-100 company decided it would allow team members to reward each other. The company's management understood that even team leaders do not really know how much each member contributes to team success. This corporation promised the team reward money if it successfully accomplished its mission. Rewards varied from a few hundred dollars to several thousand dollars, and were allocated by the team members to themselves. The system worked like so: With a five-person team and a reward sum of $500, if all members believe they contributed equally, each would get $100. However, if everyone on the team believes that two people did most of the work, they might allocate $200 to each of them and divide the remaining $100 among the other three members.

This best practice is most effective with monetary rewards—in fact, most rewards and perquisites are monetary in nature even though they may not come in the form of actual currency. Rewards may be issued as gift certificates, comp time, a driver and car for a week, and so forth. A "most-valuable team-member award" given to the team to allocate might consist of, say, three gift certificates, one for $100, one for $50, and one for $25. The team could then consider who was the most effective member, who was next best, and who was third. Or it could give the full $175 to one star player. Whatever the team decides, it has ownership of the decision and therefore cannot complain about an unfair rewards system.

- *Rewarding-Individual-Team-Members Process Best Team Practice 5: Recognize and reward support personnel.*

I'd been working at one company for a little more than a year when, during a conversation at the coffee wagon about managing support staff, my boss asked me whether I knew the name of the security guard who scanned our badges each day as we entered the office building. I answered that although I always greeted the guard with a friendly "How's it going?" I did not know his name. This particular boss was known for making his point without wasting words, so I thought quickly about what he could have meant by the question.

It only took a second for me to realize that, for more than a year, I had been passing someone doing a job that enabled me to do my job and I'd never taken the time to learn his name. My boss's point was clear: *Everyone* whose work intersects even tangentially with my work is important to my success. A person does not need to work in, for, or with my business unit to make a contribution to my ability to conduct my business. In that split second, I understood that people need to take the time to recognize the contribution every other person makes.

On my way in the next morning, I introduced myself to the guard, asked his name, and thanked him for the job he was doing. Each workday thereafter (until I transferred to a different location),

I greeted him with a smile and a "How's it going, Harry?" followed by an exchange of family news, car talk, or a few pithy observations about the favorite team.

There are many ways to familiarize oneself with another's contribution. I've heard that Fred Smith, CEO of Federal Express (at least at the time of this writing), has lunch on a regular basis in the company cafeteria. It's not because the food is great (although it may be); he eats there because it gives him time to get to know employees. If a CEO can make time in his presumably busy schedule to interact with every level of employee, IT team members should be able to take the time to recognize and reward the contribution made by the people who support team activities.

The significant role support staff can play in a team's success surprises many organizations. Secretaries and administrative assistants can produce reports that are more readable and better organized than the data from which they work. Cleaning staff can differentiate between important documents to be saved and trash to be hauled away even when messy displays of both are left helter-skelter around offices and workstations. Other "support" staff—clerical workers, drivers, messengers, paralegals, the copy shop manager down the street, and so on—contribute specific skills or work overtime to enable teams to finish projects. All help a team achieve its objective, and all should be recognized and rewarded. While teams may not have the resources to reward support staff with anything of significant monetary value, they can write letters to the person's boss recognizing a job well done, they can invite contributors to share in a team lunch, they can commend them publicly at company meetings, or they can just shake hands and thank them for their help.

Impediments to the Individual-Team-Member-Rewards Challenge

Individual team members are sometimes difficult to reward. Sometimes, no one will notice what contribution a specific team member has made. Sometimes, an individual's work is overvalued and the reward alienates or de-motivates others whose contribution has been overlooked. Sometimes, the reward available to give to an individual is in no way commensurate with the work done. So, leaders must find ways to get around such impediments.

Reward is especially difficult to calibrate when the full extent of contribution by an individual team member is not known. An act as fundamental as ordering office supplies for a department requires someone's effort but may not garner anyone else's notice. When people are assigned to a team, they typically participate in team activities, sub-team activities, and solitary activities. When all members of the team work as a team, contributions of members can be easily determined, but when a subset of a team works independently, the contribution of individuals may not be known. Because many people are reluctant to mention that they spent nights and weekends attempting to develop a solution for a team problem, their contribution may go unrecognized.

Another consideration when rewarding individuals is that doing so may alienate those not rewarded. As discussed previously in other contexts, if individual team members are going to be rewarded for individual work, then there has to be a high degree of certainty that the individual actually did that work, and that it made a major contribution to the work of the team. It's a no-brainer to conclude that if management rewards an individual for spending a lot of personal time on some aspect of a project that the team knows did not contribute to team success, then those not rewarded conceivably could and should feel alienated.

The vexing problem, as previously noted, is that the reward given an individual may not be commensurate with the work that individual performs. Assuming availability of both a team reward and a reward for individuals, rewards may be distributed so that those making the greatest contribution get the greatest rewards. It would seem obvious that if a team is given a $500 bonus per member and an individual on that team who has made an outstanding contribution is only given an additional $25, that sum may not be viewed as adequate.

Strategies to Overcome the Individual–Team–Member–Rewards Challenge

Overcoming impediments to appropriately rewarding individual team members for personal contributions to teamwork can be daunting, but there are strategies to try. The team leader can begin by documenting each team member's specific assignments. At the end of team activities, he or she can laud each team member's contribution in one-on-one meetings. Third, he or she can make certain that rewards are commensurate to contribution. The following paragraphs further explore these three steps.

By objectively recording and rating individual performance, team leaders can determine merit for compensation. Leaders must determine how to evaluate the quality of the work at completion of a task; follow-up is needed to assure that the results of that task match the success criteria for that task. If the leader is not willing to dedicate time and effort to this task, it is unlikely that attempts to reward individuals will be satisfactory.

At the end of team activities, team leaders can conduct a one-on-one critique with each team member assessing his or her contribution to the project. To minimize the risk of alienating team members, leaders can encourage team members to participate in evaluating their own effort. This approach approximates a performance appraisal for team members. Obviously, this is not an effective method unless individuals know specifically what they were to accomplish, and how that accomplishment would be measured.

Making reward commensurate to an individual's contribution means keeping the reward on scale in relationship to others' rewards. There is an easy way to do this: Suppose that one team member performed, say, 80 percent of the work and received an eight-hundred-dollar reward, give the remaining team members a maximum of two hundred dollars to share. Rewards should reflect as closely as possible the actual contribution each person makes.

Individual–Team–Member–Rewards Plan of Action

How and whether individuals are rewarded is an organization's decision to make. In some organizations, it is against policy to grant monetary rewards, but instead, they encourage individuals to show appreciation for the accomplishments of others. Other organizations reward successful teams, but do not single out individual contributors. I feel this practice is ill-advised because, in their attempt to encourage teamwork, such organizations miss out on important opportunities to motivate workers. Team leaders who believe that both individuals and teams like to be rewarded for the work they do should consider the following elements:

- rewards to individuals for their teamwork
- rewards to the entire team for its success
- rewards to team members for individual performance

Generally, in business, it is easier to evaluate the effectiveness of the team as a whole than it is to assess contributions by individual members on the team. In the wide world of sports, assessing an individual's contribution rarely appears to be a problem. Those who perform best usually get the most money. The same concept could be applied to evaluating an individual IT team member's performance, but it is sometimes harder to spot who performs best.

13

The Ultimate Team Challenge: Keeping Teamwork Competitive

During the past thirty years, the list of the largest corporations in the United States has changed dramatically. Some companies— Enron and WorldCom, for example—rose to the top and then imploded. Other companies, especially those among the U.S. automakers, have slipped down or off the list, while companies that no one had dreamed about when I first entered business, such as Amazon and Google, are at or near the top of the list.

If you were to look around the community where you live, you would see that many businesses that enjoyed success a few years ago no longer exist. Foods once considered healthy we now know to be harmful. The only constant is change. This applies to teamwork as well: What was considered a world-class team practice a few years ago may now be obsolete. For example, not too long ago, many teams met in a conference room or lunchroom to conduct team business. Now, many teams include people from different parts of the world and different business organizations who "meet" electronically. Webinars and video conferencing are commonplace. There is even a trend called the "*un*conference," where people meet without any set agenda.

Throughout my work life, I have bet my future on the competence of my company's management. If management could keep my organization competitive, I had a job for the foreseeable future. On the other hand, if management was unable to keep up with our competition, I understood that I could be laid off. The same factor functions at the industry level: The number of computer programmers in the United States, for example, has decreased as companies outsource software development to offshore contractors who presumably can do the work more effectively and cheaper.

Even if you, today, follow and implement the best practices detailed in this book, your team may not be competitive tomorrow. While it is difficult to predict team practices that will emerge in the next few years, I base my beliefs about future practices on what my interaction with hundreds of team participants has identified: Organizations continuously will look for new practices *to improve teamwork.*

Keeping Teamwork Competitive Is As Simple As 1, 2, 3

While CEO of the Quality Assurance Institute, I proposed that organizations adopt a three-step process to stay competitive in all aspects of their business, as follows:

- Step 1: Establish your baseline of team performance (reflecting current teamwork performance).
- Step 2: Define your teamwork goal (to maintain teamwork competitiveness and achieve world-class team performance).
- Step 3: Develop a plan to move from your baseline to your goal.

Step 1: Establish your baseline of team performance.

You completed this step by filling out the team effectiveness self-assessment workpaper, Workpaper #1, included in Chapter 1. This self-assessment and the team effectiveness footprint provide an overall evaluation.

Now that you have read in detail about the top-ten challenges to teamwork, fill out the self-assessment workpaper again. You will probably respond differently because of a better understanding of the intent of the fifty self-assessment questions. This second stab at self-assessment should serve as a baseline for team performance.

Step 2: Define your teamwork goal.

Your goal for teamwork should be to score 100 points on the self-assessment workpaper. In today's competitive workplace, this would put you at world-class status. Even a score in the 90s would make you world-class.

While implementing the best team practices in your organization, you also need to consider *emerging* best team practices. Successful teams will incorporate emerging best practices into team processes and self-assessments. The top-ten challenges to teamwork will change.

Step 3: Develop a plan to move from your baseline to your goal.

I worked at one point as a consultant to a large organization that was trying to improve the architecture of its software. It developed a software-architecture rating system and mandated that the project manager use it. Based on the rating, the project manager could then bid for resources to improve certain components of the software. For example, if the project manager rated adequacy of the architecture as a 2 out of 5 ("5" being the highest rating), this would justify a bid for resources to improve that aspect of the software. At the conclusion of the improvement cycle, the project manager would again rate the software, which, if improved to a 3 or higher, would elevate the project to be deemed successful.

I asked management why it allowed a current project manager to rate the state of his or her own software, to set an improvement goal, and to rate the software after improvement. This unreliable, presumably preferential, rating system distressed me: Couldn't the project manager just *say* that adequacy moved from a 2 to a 3, whether it did or not? Management's answer was eye-opening: Its real objective was to focus the project manager's sights on improving the architecture of the software. Management didn't care about the rating system; it just wanted improvement.

Emerging Team Practices

To identify emerging team practices, I surveyed literally hundreds of team members. The ten emerging team practices detailed below are in place, effectively practiced, somewhere. A caveat, however: For the most part, these practices remain the province of rare, nimble organizations. Some team practices may work only in certain business cultures while others may be readily adopted by almost all organizations relying on teams.

1. *Forensic analysis:* Teams are applying forensic-analysis techniques to work processes to identify areas of weakness. This methodical analysis investigates each part of a process to determine whether a problem exists and, if it exists, with which process component it is associated. Process components include input, work procedures, check procedures, tools, people, environment, deliverables, and more.

2. *Team composition:* Teams are being formed by anyone who determines there is a problem that could best be addressed by a team (although, in fact, many businesses still give authority to managers alone to form teams). Anyone can appoint a team, and any staff member, regardless of his or her position in the organization, can select people appropriate for the team. No management authorization is needed under this emerging best team practice.

3. *Team leadership:* An emerging team practice is that teams themselves elect their leader. This practice builds on the premise that members of a team are in a better position to appoint a team leader than management. If team members appoint their own leader, they are generally more willing to listen to and work for him or her than for a leader management has appointed.

4. *Global teamwork:* As we move more toward a world economy, the number of transnational teams increases. Years ago, when I worked on a worldwide software system, stakeholders traveled to different countries to attend meetings and to install systems. Modern communication technology renders that type of travel unnecessary. Factors that foster successful global teamwork include the following:

    - continuous communication among team members

- rules to govern teamwork
- team member roles and responsibilities defined in multinational terms
- team-building exercises
- team missions defined in measurable terms

5. *Change techniques:* Emerging team practices encourage creativity by teaching principles of innovation. Innovation techniques free people from thinking about ways to improve what is currently *in place* to thinking instead about radical change, focusing on breakthrough goals. Toyota, for example, invited engineers to design an automobile with half the number of parts of current models.

6. *Visualization:* Sports psychologists, in working with professional athletes unable to perform some aspect of the position they play, train the athletes to *visualize doing* the something they cannot do. For example, golfers are taught to visualize exactly the shot they want to make before they attempt to make it. If team members can visualize the result they want to accomplish in their organization, they are better equipped to reach that team objective. Team leaders, at the least, should be able to visualize goals and results, but the more members of a team that can visualize achieving goals and results, the higher the probability of a project's success.

7. *Social-network analysis:* Another emerging team practice uses social-network analysis to pick team leaders. By creating a node diagram showing the relationships between individual team members, everyone can clearly see whom the team members respect most and can appoint that individual as team leader. The node diagram eliminates open-ended discussion, debate, and votes among team members.

8. *Created space:* The era of the leader as someone who walks into a room filled with team members, takes charge, and determines all activities and direction is no longer the desired norm. Today's teams are composed of members in distant parts of the world, collocated people who need to telecommute to virtual meetings in order to interact on a continuous basis. Leaders need to create

space in which all members can operate. MySpace, created in cyberspace for individuals to out personal information and desires or to glean secrets and ambitions from strangers, exemplifies just such wildly successful, created space. Not to be outdone, the United States Army has a Website that allows a large group of Army members to communicate in real-time and learn from others' challenges and experiences. This form of sharing space and communicating experiences fosters team community.

9. *Compliance conundrum:* Many organizations today are overly engaged in complying with a variety of rules, regulations, and laws, rather than focusing on greater productivity and quality breakthroughs. Even when teams establish their own rules, organizations have standards with which all solutions must comply. The solution to breaking the compliance conundrum is to free team members from all compliance concerns until they develop a recommended solution. Only then can they conduct a second investigation regarding compliance to rules, regulations, and laws.

10. *Rules of engagement:* Similar to establishing a Code of Ethics for a team, which tends to deal primarily with values and vision, rules of engagement focus on interaction between team members. Organizations that establish rules of engagement such as the following for their teams are likely to be better prepared to meet the demands of the future:

- Challenge the issue, not the person.
- Consider all options.
- Stand up for your position, but never argue against the facts.
- Allow yourself the opportunity to give serious consideration to opposing views.
- Lose the words "I" and "they" once a decision is reached.

Final Thoughts on Putting the "I" Back into Team

As you prepare to employ the fifty building blocks for best team practices, consider the following overarching concepts to help improve your organization.

Believing versus expecting: When you work hard and complete tasks assigned to you, on time and within budget, you may *believe* that you'll be rewarded with promotion. But believing that you will be promoted does not require you to take any specific action: You are waiting for an event to happen to you rather than taking action to make it happen.

Expecting to be promoted is significantly different. If you expect to be promoted, you might start dressing for the job you expect to get. If you expect to be promoted, you might start learning new skills for the position you expect to have. If you expect to be promoted, you might start thinking about the work you expect to do when promoted.

Expecting is proactive. Believing, by itself, does not lead to action. If you *believe* that teams could do better than they are currently doing in your organization, you do not have to take any action. However, if you *expect* teams to perform better, you need to begin preparing an environment and a culture in which more-effective, more-efficient teamwork can thrive.

Designed for individuals who *expect* that teams can be more effective and more efficient in the future, this book has offered the tools; now is the time for you to be proactive. Become the "I" who holds the key to effective, efficient teamwork, the leader taking good and great teams to world-class status, and, drawing final inspiration from our many sports-team analogies, the cheerleader who chants for change:

- **I will help change teamwork attitudes.**
- **I will work to change team process.**
- **I will initiate change.**
- **I will champion effective teamwork.**
- **If it's going to be, it's up to me.**

Index

Acceptance criteria, 12, 39, 79, 82ff. *See also* Entrance criteria; Exit criteria; Requirements.
Accountability, 28, 35, 38, 43ff., 60, 92-93, 112, 128
Accounting, department, 81, 88ff., 91-92
    illegal practices, 59
    process, 81, 85-86, 88
Action, 8, 10, 32-33, 45-46, 57, 66, 76-77, 86-87, 96, 105, 106, 114, 123-24
    blaming, 65, 70-71
    consensus, 52, 60, 98, 101
    doing, *xiii*, 25, 30ff., 42, 65, 92-93, 106
    reward &, 115-24, 131
    success &, *xii*, 10, 52, 62, 106, 112, 131
Adams, Scott, 19*n*.
Agenda, 26, 38, 40, 111, 125
    hidden, 7, 49, 53, 59-60, 75
Analysis, 78-79, 94, 128, 129
Appreciations, 117, 120-21, 123
Assigned task
    constraints &, 36, 40, 44, 75
    opposing, 53, 55, 61, 74-75, 90
    performing, 9, 10, 13, 17, 26, 29-31, 34, 37, 42-43, 44, 45-46, 47ff., 49, 57, 61, 67ff., 86-87, 89, 94, 108ff., 111, 112, 115, 122, 131
Attribute, 4, 17, 34, 39, 109
Authority, 13, 25-26, 29, 32, 38, 55, 86, 88, 90, 92-93, 94ff., 128
    limit on, 13, 41-42, 48, 92-93
    situational, 92-93

Baseball team, 5-6, 68, 74-75, 91, 108-9, 115, 117. *See also* Coaching; Sports team; Yankees.
Believing versus expecting, 131
Benefit. *See also* Reward.
    financial, 107, 112, 118
    individual, 39, 52-53, 55-56, 63, 66, 70, 73, 75, 76, 87, 92ff., 96, 111, 118, 131
    organizational, 48, 56, 70, 75, 76, 87, 89, 94-96, 111-12, 131

supervisory, 75, 76
    team, 61, 66, 70, 75, 104, 111
Best team practices, *xii, xiv,* 18, 27ff., 37ff., 51ff., 61ff., 69ff., 82ff., 91ff., 100ff., 118ff., 125ff., 131
Brainstorming, *xiv,* 36, 43, 48
Budget
    consideration, 28, 39, 51, 57, 95, 107, 111
    as constraint, 51, 72, 113, 131
Business. *See also* Silo; Vendor.
    culture, 3, 16, 18, 42, 62, 97ff., 111-12, 125, 127, 128, 130
    human factor in, *xi-xii,* 4, 21, 35, 43, 48, 50, 68, 88ff., 97, 111-12, 117, 119, 120
    objective, 7-8, 14, 50, 70, 72, 93, 94-95, 126-27
    problem-solving &, 3, 4ff., 17, 18, 26, 48, 85ff., 106, 126, 127, 130
    team &, 4-6, 16ff., 25, 54, 61, 68, 74, 87, 97, 119-20, 124, 125
Business team, 4-9, 15, 17, 35, 53, 88ff. *See also* Silo; Team.
    cast of characters, 4, 6-7, 18, 41-42
    defined, 4*n.*, 72
    individual on, 5, 6, 31-32, 35, 40, 43, 47, 48-49, 51-52, 54, 68, 69, 70, 74, 85, 98, 121
    model, 43, 50, 52, 61, 70
    role on, *xi,* 3, 4, 6-7, 10, 11, 25, 28, 30, 41-42, 74
    weakness of, 6, 15, 17, 97ff., 117
Buy-in, 91, 98-99

Career, 29, 42, 50-51, 71, 112, 125
    building, 35, 57, 131
    opportunity in, 35, 131
Challenges, *xiv,* 4, 7, 9, 10-14, 15, 16, 18, 19ff., 37, 46, 51, 56, 72, 83, 111, 113, 126, 127, 130
Change, *xi-xii, xiv,* 20, 90, 95, 108, 117, 125, 127, 129, 131
    implementing, 13, 28, 90, 94-96, 98, 102, 105, 109-10, 111-12, 131

133

Chart
    recognition, 119
    team-effectiveness, 15-16, 126
Checklist
    anti-groupthink, 13, 100, 102
    back-up plan, 54, 96
Coaching, 5, 10, 12, 25, 27, 29, 32, 40, 45, 48,
        53, 54, 58, 70, 72, 100, 117. *See also*
        Sports team.
    baseball, 5, 68, 74, 75, 91, 108-9, 115, 117
    Dream Team & NBA, 58, 64
    football, 25, 26, 27, 40, 42, 43, 47-48, 54,
        68, 70, 73-74, 117
    Herb Brooks & ice hockey, 58, 61
    Lou Holtz & football, 47
    NFL, 27, 35, 44, 70, 73
    Pop Warner football, 42
    Tom Landry & Dallas Cowboys, 26-27,
        35, 43-44, 70, 73
Code, programming, 44
Code of Ethics, 11, 61-62, 130
Communication, 36, 84, 86, 125ff.
Compensation, 22, 118, 123, 124. *See also*
        Reward; Salary.
Competitiveness, 20, 43, 47, 119, 125-31
    three-step process, 126
Compliance conundrum, 130
Consensus, 18, 31, 59-60, 69, 73, 97-99, 100,
        104, 105
Constraint, *xiv*, 36, 45, 51
    budgetary, 44, 51, 57, 85, 104, 111, 113,
        131
Consultant, 20, 54, 110-11, 127
Contract, *xiv*, 6, 39, 89
    with stakeholder, *xiv*, 78-87
Control, 6-7, 12, 18, 73-74, 81, 111
Creative thinking & artist story, 21-22
Creativity, 3, 21-22, 36, 45, 50-51, 129
Crosby, Philip B., *xi-xii*
Culture, 97ff., 128, 131
    in business, 3, 17, 128
    democratic aspect of, 16, 18, 25-26, 41-
        42, 48
    difference in, 77
Customer, 12, 62, 78-87, 102, 114. *See also*
        Stakeholder; User.
    acceptance criteria &, 12, 39, 79, 82ff.
    categories of, 81
    core, 66
    on focus group, 84
    identifying, 78-81, 86-87
    management as, 81
    restaurant analogy, 79-80
    satisfaction, 78ff., 85-86, 112
    survey, 12, 82-83
    voice of, 12, 23, 24, 78-87, 102, 113
    work site, 12, 83-84

Data gathering, *xii, xiii*, 22, 34, 58, 63, 71, 73,
        78, 79, 82, 83, 84, 91, 93ff., 121
    human aspect in, 41, 62, 111, 130
    survey &, 83

Decision-making, 3, 10, 13, 21, 25-26, 29, 48,
        68, 69, 71, 78ff., 91-92, 98ff., 100-3,
        104, 111, 112, 130
    by consensus, 59-60, 97ff., 120, 123
    judicial, 100-101
    tainted, 97ff.
Defect, 38, 63, 93, 97, 99
    common cause, 73-74
    hardware, 21, 88-89, 93
    software, *xi-xii*, 21*n.*, 93, 94
    special cause, 73-74
Deliverable, *xiii*, 12, 39-40, 45, 46, 54, 77ff.,
        82, 83, 84, 85, 93-94, 102, 128, 129.
        See also Product.
Deming, W. Edwards, 73
Department, 81, 85, 92, 94. *See also* Silo.
    accounting, 81, 86, 88, 92
    hierarchy, 88, 90, 92
    human resources, 26
    IT, 3, 28, 42, 78, 88ff., 95-96, 101, 108,
        109, 111, 114, 121, 124
    purchasing, 88, 90, 91, 94, 95, 122
    support, 13, 28, 38, 55, 76, 88ff., 91, 92,
        103, 105
Documentation, 8, 39, 50, 116, 121, 122
Double-cut theory. *See* Skunk-works.

Entrance criteria, 10, 11, 23, 24, 34-46, 51, 82,
        83, 114
    management &, 35-36, 43, 71
    measurability of, 39-40, 71
    team, 32, 35-36, 38, 40-42, 49, 68, 82
Example
    automobile, 21, 85-86, 129
    basketball free-throw, 40, 117
    bike riding, 67, 72
    butterfly life-cycle, *xiii-xiv*
    buy-in, 98-99
    cake-baking, 34
    cookie-ingredients, 38
    Dallas Cowboys, 26-27, 35, 43-44, 70, 73
    Dream Team, 58, 64
    Federal Express CEO, 121
    Glenn Miller & band, 50, 52
    house, 40, 82, 113
    IBM's costly investment, 63
    insurance agent, 78ff., 81, 85
    lawnmower selection, 81
    left-brain, 21-22
    lightbulb invention, 36, 119
    newspaper test, 19-20
    Notre Dame football, 47
    Olympics, 58
    payroll system, 48
    Pop Warner football, 42
    Roderique, the Wonder Dog, 67
    room cleaning, 36-37
    security guard, 120-21
    self-initiated luck, 19, 20
    six-sigma, 21
    software-architecture, 127
    South Pacific lyric, 97
    Thomas Edison, 36, 106, 119

Toyota design challenge, 45, 129
traffic laws, 44
"Two Sheets and a Blanket," 60
Walt Disney turnaround, 62
Yankees' uniform, 108-9
Exit criteria, 10, 11, 12, 23, 24, 34-46, 50, 51, 53, 54, 82, 85, 97, 113, 123. *See also* Acceptance criteria;Entrance criteria; Requirements.
Expectation, 38, 68, 109, 131
customer, 39, 80, 84, 113
team, 56, 61
Expert, subject-matter, 4, 54, 74, 92

Facilitating, 12, 25, 26, 64, 69, 84
Failure, 38, 60, 72, 106
computer systems, 87-88
as learning tool, *xi*, 36, 119
performance, *xiv*, 4, 11, 17, 23, 28, 38, 75, 97-98, 101, 113, 114
preventing, 50, 72-73, 106ff.
rewarding, 11, 35, 63-64, 70
taking responsibility for, 43, 44, 45, 108, 112, 118-19
Feature, 78ff., 83, 85, 98
Focal team, 8-9, 15-16, 18
Functionality, 7-8, 25, 31-32, 41, 62, 79-80, 92, 98, 103-4
Future team, 3, 15, 18, 125-31

Global teamwork, 78, 125, 128-30, 131
Goal
achieving, 38, 51, 55, 59, 66, 69, 77, 80, 87, 89, 109-10, 112, 114, 127, 129
business, 7, 14, 21*n*., 36, 70, 80, 86, 89, 95-96, 125ff.
communicating, 6, 37, 85, 127
customer expectation as, 80, 110
identifying, *xiii*, 6, 7, 34, 36, 44, 66, 69ff., 106ff., 126, 127, 129
individual, 6, 12, 25, 26, 31, 35, 49, 64, 69ff., 70, 74, 106ff., 112, 126ff.
management, 32, 35, 55, 109, 127
project, 14, 26, 39-41, 43, 65, 74, 75, 89, 110
pursuing, 7, 14, 37, 43, 67, 74, 77, 89, 102, 106ff., 111, 126, 131
team, *xiii*, 6, 7, 8, 12, 14, 26, 30, 35, 37, 38, 40, 44, 53, 55, 57, 64, 69, 70, 77, 80ff., 89, 101, 106ff., 110-11, 121, 126ff., 129
undermining, 7, 49, 53, 59, 64, 65, 70, 74, 90
visualized, 8, 45, 129
Group dynamic, 3, 19, 60, 66, 74, 77, 84, 97ff., 103, 119-20, 128-30
Groupthink, 3, 5, 13, 97-105
anti-groupthink checklist, 13, 102
avoiding, 13, 23, 24, 97-105
benefits of, 99-100
consensus &, 99-100, 103-4
mob psychology &, 3, 88, 98

Hardware, 28, 88-89, 110, 111
Hawthorne tests, 73. *See also* Quality.
Hierarchy, 33, 35, 88-93. *See also* Silo.
Hopper, Grace, 93
Human factor, 111

Implementation
ineffective, 9, 21, 97, 108
practices, 69, 71, 100, 126
project, 114
software, 78, 85-86, 127, 128
of solution, 3, 14, 21, 75, 94, 102, 105, 108ff., 114
Individual
commitment, 6, 27, 30, 91, 112
creativity &, 3, 21-22, 28, 36, 45
motivating, 5, 17, 25ff., 31, 33, 42-43, 52, 53, 61, 64, 69-70, 84, 99, 108ff., 112, 115-24
reward &, 6, 12, 14, 23, 24, 32, 49, 56-57, 61, 68, 69-71, 95, 96, 101, 115-24
on team, 3, 6-7, 10, 11, 13, 25, 27, 28, 29-30, 31-32, 35, 40, 42-43, 48, 51-52, 54, 55-56, 58, 60, 64, 66, 68, 72-73, 75, 76-77, 91, 92, 98, 99, 104, 106, 108, 119, 129
Industry, 62, 70, 111, 114, 119, 125, 128
Information-gathering, *xiii*, 22, 34ff., 71, 79ff., 83-84, 86, 87
Information technology (IT), 3, 28, 42, 78, 88ff., 96, 101, 108, 109, 111, 114, 124
Innovation, 3, 14, 21-22, 36-37, 119, 129
Integration, 108, 128
Integrity, *xiv*, 11, 59, 62-63, 65-66. *See also* Code of Ethics.

Job description, 26, 32-33, 70-71, 91-92
Job performance, 11, 29, 30, 36-37, 41-42, 49, 51, 53, 67ff., 70-71, 88-89, 92-93, 98-99, 103, 112-13. *See also* Performance evaluation.
appraisal of, 26, 30, 32, 55, 71, 75, 89, 118, 123-24
failure in, 6, 30, 36-37, 47, 74, 108, 119
in hierarchy, 31, 41-42, 88ff.
improving, 13, 15, 26, 29, 40-41, 67ff., 90, 103, 108-9, 115-24, 126ff., 131
motivation &, 6, 26, 30-32, 36-37, 42-43, 55, 70, 108-9, 112, 115, 118, 123
programming in the U. S., 97, 125
success &, 5-6, 31, 55, 100, 106-7, 123
Judicial process, 100-2

Knowledge, 22, 26, 30, 40, 42, 43, 48, 56, 65, 69, 77-78, 85-86, 91, 108, 120, 122

Landry, Tom, 26-27, 35, 43-44, 70, 73. *See also* Coaching.
Law, *xiv*, 20*n*., 21-22, 44, 81, 130. *See also* Rule.

Leadership, 18, 23, 24, 25-33, 38, 48, 51-57, 58, 61, 62-63, 64, 65-66, 68, 69, 71ff., 76, 84ff., 89ff., 98-99, 103, 104, 105, 107, 108, 109, 113, 114, 117, 118, 122, 123, 128, 131
Learning, *xi, xiii,* 20, 31, 42, 51, 54, 60, 66, 67, 69, 73, 74, 92, 95, 97, 111, 115, 116, 119, 126, 131. *See also* Training.
  experience, *xi,* 47, 60, 79, 130
  kids &, 5, 36-37, 42, 67, 74-75, 115
  new technology &, 21, 111, 131
  reward &, 67, 115, 119, 131

Management
  in business, *xi-xii,* 3, 7, 25, 39, 48, 68, 74, 80, 88ff., 95-96, 98-99, 110-11, 117, 120, 121, 125, 127, 128
  commitment, 38, 41, 46, 57, 62, 69, 90, 108ff., 114, 128
  cooperation, 14, 32, 41, 46, 55, 61, 74, 87, 90, 92-93, 95-96, 102, 110ff., 128
  as customer, 81, 84
  opposition, 55, 74, 93, 107, 113
  responsibility, 5-6, 28, 31, 33, 35, 43-45, 46, 62, 87, 110-14, 125, 127, 128
  senior, 35, 43, 44, 80, 87, 88, 95, 100, 111, 117
  sports, 5-6, 25, 26, 28, 41, 42, 44, 47, 70
  task, 4, 8, 17, 26, 80, 112, 127
  team &, 3, 6, 8, 14, 17, 25ff., 36ff., 47, 49, 61, 68, 95-96, 117, 119, 122
  tone at the top, 59, 62, 120
Management By Walking Around, 110-11
Measurability, 39-40, 71, 123, 129
Meetings, 3-5, 6-7, 8, 38, 41, 49, 71, 75, 85, 86, 111, 121, 123, 125, 128-29
  rules for, *xiv,* 7, 38, 40, 61, 65, 71, 104
Method, *xiv,* 3-18, 28, 36-37, 39, 43, 83, 86, 90, 96, 100-101, 103, 119
  changing, 21, 54, 64
  conflict resolution, 43, 48, 80, 91, 100ff., 109
Mission. *See also* Silo.
  accomplishing, *xiii-xiv,* 9, 13, 16, 17, 18, 20, 26, 30-32, 34, 38, 42, 43, 51, 55, 65, 67, 70, 76-77, 85-86, 89, 90ff., 94-95, 96, 104, 109, 111, 119, 129
  preparing for, 23, 26, 42, 66, 74, 76, 96, 97, 103
  statement, 69, 86, 96
  support for, 7-8, 13, 14, 55, 59, 66, 76-77, 84, 86, 91, 93, 94, 95-96, 98, 101, 104, 110, 121, 127
Model for World-Class Teamwork, 23, 24
More Secrets of Consulting, 20*n.*
Motivation, 17, 23, 27, 28, 30, 31, 32, 37, 52-56, 106, 109, 115ff.

National Basketball Association (NBA). *See* Coaching; Sports team.
National Football League (NFL). *See* Coaching; Sports team.

Objective
  individual, *xii,* 6, 25, 35, 37, 43, 64, 69, 70, 71, 72
  organizational, 7, 21*n.,* 35, 36, 45, 70, 74, 77, 80, 89, 109-10, 111, 127, 129
  team, *xiii,* 7, 8, 14, 26, 30, 34, 37, 38, 44, 51, 53, 55, 57, 59, 64, 65, 66, 69, 70, 83, 86, 87, 89, 101, 110, 121, 126, 127, 129
Observation
  by managers, 55, 74, 110-11, 127
  mistakes in, 91-92, 121
  on-site, 12, 25, 42, 74, 83-84, 122
  power of, 20, 121
Organization. *See also* Business; Silo.
  accounting, 59, 81, 85-86, 88-89, 91, 92
  actual, 14, 17, 78, 91-92
  diagramming, 13, 91-92, 129
  formal, 10, 17, 33, 35, 41-42, 49-50, 57, 61, 67, 87, 91-92, 119, 123, 126, 130
  IT department, 28, 29, 31, 42, 88-89, 96, 101, 108, 111, 121, 124
  purchasing, 23, 35, 88ff., 90, 91, 94, 95-96, 97, 128
  structure, 18, 26, 31, 47, 76, 88ff., 121, 125-26
Outsourcing, 111-12, 125

Peer pressure, 97ff., 101, 103, 105. *See also* Groupthink.
Peers, 3, 21-22, 60, 66, 77, 84, 103, 105, 115, 118ff., 130
Performance evaluation, 6, 13, 17, 26, 27, 28, 30, 31-33, 34ff., 38, 48, 49, 55ff., 68, 70, 71, 73, 74, 75, 89, 94, 102-3, 109, 116, 118, 123-24, 131
Planning, *xiii-xiv,* 5, 6, 8, 12, 17, 27, 32ff., 39, 43, 45ff., 54, 57ff., 60, 66ff., 71-72, 76ff., 84, 86ff., 94, 96, 97, 99-100, 104, 105, 106ff., 109, 114, 123-24, 126, 127
Problem solving, 3-18, 22, 26, 36-37, 62, 63, 65, 84, 88-89, 94, 107, 109-10, 122, 128, 130
  ineffective, 5, 17, 18, 64, 108, 122
  identifying, 7, 17, 18, 44, 59, 84, 109, 124, 128
  left-brain vs. right, 21, 36
Procedure
  establishing, *xiv,* 10, 36-37, 40, 43, 44, 46, 49-50, 61, 119
  work, 50, 128
Process, 13, 15, 22, 28, 95, 100-2, 128
  challenge to, 15, 46, 55-57, 88, 90, 95, 96, 103-4, 127, 131
  decision-making, 26, 36, 68, 100-101
  defining criteria, 37, 43, 82
  formal, 37, 46, 50, 82-83, 87, 89
  improvement, *xii,* 22, 37, 45, 106-14, 119, 127
  leadership, 27-31
  listening to voice of customer, 78-87
  rewards, 115-24

selection, 11, 47-57, 68, 75
in silos, 88-96
training, 67-77
trust-building, 58-66
Product. *See also* Deliverable.
build, *xiii*, 45, 51, 83, 93-94
designer, 39, 78ff.
feature, 12, 78ff., 85, 93, 127
software, 28, 39, 79, 84-85
Productivity, 8, 34, 36, 42, 45, 64, 119, 121, 128, 130
Project
budget, 39, 72, 75, 107, 113
failure, 10, 28, 50, 63, 97, 106ff., 113-14
goal, 14, 43, 44, 51, 65, 74, 106-7, 109-10, 112, 114, 121, 127
management, 22, 26, 39, 54, 72, 92, 106, 107, 110-11, 112, 114, 117, 127
planning, *xiv*, 26, 39, 44, 72, 99-100, 106-7, 110, 113, 122, 123
resource, 74, 106-7
scope, 112, 128-30

Quality, *xi-xii*, 17, 35, 37, 55, 63, 69, 73, 93, 95, 98, 106, 115, 123, 129
coach, 12, 73-74, 81
cost of, 93-94, 111-12, 119-20
improving, 87, 112, 119, 130
of information, 71, 73, 74, 93
measuring, 29, 71, 89, 93-94, 116, 119-20
Quality Assurance Institute (QAI), *xii*, 29, 113, 126

Rat-hole theory. *See* Skunk-works.
Recommendation, 13, 95-96, 100, 102, 103, 104, 112. *See also* Reward.
implementing, 14, 48, 94, 102, 104, 109, 112
support for, 59, 98-99, 101, 102, 105, 108, 111, 112
Recruiting, 5, 11, 52-54, 56ff., 64, 66, 68
Reengineering, 3-18
Requirements, 11, 17, 28, 39-40, 44, 46, 48, 54, 60ff., 78ff., 94, 95, 100, 107, 113, 116, 118, 122, 131. *See also* Acceptance criteria; Entrance criteria; Exit criteria.
customer, 78ff., 85, 113
gathering, 79ff., 83, 85, 87
Resource, 17, 18, 22, 26, 38-39, 54, 86, 106ff., 114
securing, 43, 44, 45, 57, 60, 69, 76, 102, 107, 109, 113, 121, 127
tracking, 76, 111
Responsibility, 10, 74, 87, 95
individual, 6, 45, 55, 70-71, 73, 107-8, 116
supervisory, 25-26, 28-29, 31, 35, 39, 44, 55, 66, 69, 70-71, 75, 92-93, 105
team, *xiv*, 6, 10, 22, 47, 57, 68, 69, 86, 108, 112, 113, 115, 129
Review, 24, 29, 31-33, 55, 86, 105, 111. *See*

also Performance evaluation.
Reward, 3, 11, 14, 17, 22, 24, 30-31, 35, 53, 56, 63-64, 67-70, 115-124
individual vs. group, 3, 6, 53, 68, 69ff., 115, 116, 117ff., 122
as motivation, 53, 69, 115ff., 121-22, 123
unearned, 11, 35, 39, 56, 63-64, 116, 121
Risk-taking, 29, 31, 63-64, 66, 72, 92-93, 123
Rule, 20-22, 39, 42, 43, 44, 46, 47, 71, 129. *See also* Law.
Rules of engagement. *See* Code of Ethics.

Schedule, 28, 39, 57, 72, 75, 103-4
Secrets of Consulting, 20*n*.
Self-analysis questionnaire, 103
Self-assessment, 4, 8-18., 123, 126, 127. *See also* Team effectiveness.
Service provider, 79ff., 93, 118
Silo, 13, 23, 24, 88-96
Skill, 4, 6, 28, 32, 33, 42-43, 48, 49, 51, 58, 66, 81, 95
administrative, 52-53, 62-63, 71, 120-21
improving, 5, 11, 25, 29-31, 40-41, 42, 47, 54, 65, 68, 69, 72, 74-75, 115ff., 129
Skunk-works, 107
Software
application, 29, 48, 79, 85, 128
budget, 28, 39, 93, 107
deliverable, 39-40, 42, 46, 54, 127
development, 28, 29, 39-40, 44, 48, 78, 79, 93-94, 113, 125-26, 127
project management, 28, 39-40, 107, 114, 127
schedule, 28, 39, 44, 57, 72
Solution, 3-18, 22, 89, 90, 108, 122. *See also* Problem-solving.
achieving, 86, 94, 98, 99ff., 108, 109-10
implementing, 21, 109ff., 114
rethinking, 21, 74, 130
Specification, 78ff. *See also* Acceptance criteria; Entrance criteria; Exit Criteria; Requirements.
Sports, *xi*, 8, 26, 27, 28, 41, 54, 100, 117, 124, 129
Sports team, 3, 4*n*., 5-6, 26ff., 30, 34, 35, 43, 68, 91, 97, 98, 100, 108-9, 116, 129, 131. *See also* Coaching; Training.
kids &, 5-6, 8, 42-43, 74-75, 115
practice, 5, 30, 34ff., 40, 47, 53, 68
professional, 6, 25, 26-27, 28, 32, 34ff., 42-43, 44, 48, 58, 70, 71-72, 108-9, 115
reward &, 6, 35, 70, 115, 117, 119
Stakeholder, *xii*, *xiv*, 13, 14, 86, 87, 94, 110, 111-12, 128. *See also* Customer; User.
Statistics, 13, 21*n*., 38, 40, 94, 107, 123
Success, 106-14
influencing, *xi*, 69ff., 74, 97-105, 107ff.
inhibiting, 20-22, 36, 51, 55, 74, 90, 92-93, 97, 106-14, 116
luck &, 20-21, 111
measuring, 39, 71

responsibility for, 5, 25ff., 34ff., 54, 66, 70, 88ff., 93, 104, 112, 129
team effort &, 58ff., 69ff., 92-93, 108, 115ff., 121ff., 128ff.
Survey, 12, 23, 82-83, 85-86, 87, 113, 127

Tasks
  accomplishing, 5, 17, 23ff., 26, 29ff., 38, 42, 51, 55, 68, 71, 72-73, 75, 76, 86, 89, 90, 92-93, 98, 104, 106ff., 112ff., 122-23, 131
  prioritizing, 4-5, 54, 61, 67, 75, 95
Team. See also Business; Business team; Coaching; Team member.
  building, 41, 50, 57, 58, 66, 68, 77, 129
  fear on, 22, 31, 55, 84, 99
  motivation, 5, 10, 14, 17, 23, 26ff., 28, 30-32, 37, 42, 52, 55, 56, 64, 67ff. 77, 103, 106, 108, 115ff., 121, 123
  nonfunctional, 7-8, 17, 18, 25, 31, 32, 41, 49, 97ff., 112-13
  participation, 3-4, 17, 49, 51, 53, 55, 56-57, 61, 66, 75, 84-85, 90, 122-23
  role on, 3ff., 10, 11, 18, 23, 28, 30, 31ff., 41-42, 47ff., 62, 69, 85, 121, 129
  scoreboard, 9, 15ff., 27-28, 119, 127
  staffing, 47ff., 54, 66, 84ff., 91, 120-21, 128
Team effectiveness, xiii-xiv, 3-5, 7, 8-17, 19ff., 25-27, 29, 32-33, 41, 45, 48, 52, 61, 67, 74, 76-77, 90, 95, 97, 100, 102-4, 111, 117-18, 124, 126, 131
Team goal, xiii, 7, 8, 14, 26, 30, 35, 36, 43, 45, 55, 64ff., 69-70, 74, 77, 89, 109-11, 126ff., 129
Team leader, 10-14, 23-24, 25ff., 74, 89-90, 93, 98-99, 103, 104, 128. See also Management.
  assistant to, 11, 54, 62-63, 66, 71
  bad vs. good, xi-xii, 27ff., 41, 72-73, 85, 93, 108-9, 117
  responsibility of, 25ff., 38, 48, 51-52, 57, 62, 65, 67, 75-76, 84, 87, 104, 105, 110, 118, 122-23, 129
  selection, 10, 11, 23-24, 25-33, 128, 129
Team meeting, 3, 38, 61, 104, 128-29
  focus group, 12, 84-85
Team member, xi, 11, 18, 47-57
  chemistry, 11, 58, 59, 62-63, 64, 66, 77
  communication skill, 84, 86, 103, 128
  recruiting, 11, 49, 50, 52ff., 56, 57, 64, 66
  responsibility, 5-6, 10, 22, 47, 54, 66, 67ff., 70-71, 86, 93, 107-8, 112, 113, 115, 116, 119ff., 129
  reward &, 3, 8, 11, 14, 17, 23, 24, 30-31, 35, 56, 63-64, 67-68, 69ff., 115-24
  selection, 6, 10, 11, 18, 23, 24, 25ff., 47-57, 64, 74, 75, 128
  staff &, 54, 62, 120-21, 128
Team mission, xiii-xiv, 9, 13, 17, 18, 20, 23, 26, 30-31, 67, 76-77, 85-87, 90-96, 97, 101, 103-4. See also Mission.
Team problem-solving, 3-18, 21, 25-26, 36,

41-42, 94, 109, 122, 125-31. See also Problem-solving.
Team training, 11, 12, 23, 24, 27-28, 29-31, 40-42, 45, 47, 51, 53-54, 56-57, 67-77, 92, 95ff., 109, 113
Teamwork, 4, 8, 19-24, 26-27, 30-33, 37-38, 44, 53, 56, 59, 68, 71-72, 77, 107-8, 116, 122-24, 125-31
Technology, xi-xii, 28, 29, 39, 42, 44, 48, 51, 78, 85-86, 88-89, 93, 97, 110, 111, 113, 114, 125, 128
Testing, 29, 39, 68, 101, 108
Thinking outside the box, 3, 21-22, 36-37, 44-45, 78-79, 129
Tool, 28, 43, 56, 88-89, 110, 119, 128, 131
Training, 11, 12, 23, 26, 27-28, 30-31, 34, 39, 40-41, 43ff., 45, 47, 49, 51, 53ff., 56, 60-63, 67-77, 82, 84, 92-93, 95, 96, 109, 113, 115, 129
  imported, 12, 26, 54, 69, 84, 91
  knowledge-based, 40, 48, 65, 91
Trend, 125, 127-30
Trust, 11, 19, 23, 24, 58-66, 84

Unconference, 125
U.S. military, 60, 130
U.S. Supreme Court, 100
User, 39, 79, 82, 86, 102, 113. See also Customer; Stakeholder.

Value, 42, 43, 53, 56, 97, 104, 117, 121, 130
Vendor, 7, 12, 21n., 72, 79ff., 88-89, 91, 118, 125, 127, 130. See also Business.
Vision, 42, 130
Visualization, 5, 6, 15, 39-40, 48, 73, 78, 107, 123, 129
Voting, 13, 18, 48-49, 100, 101-2, 119-20, 129

Weinberg, Gerald M., 20n.
What's in it for me? (WIIFM), 13, 56, 94
Work, 125-130, 131. See also Global teamwork; Teamwork.
  ethic, 8, 11, 22, 38, 39, 42-43, 59, 61-62, 64, 65-66, 70-71, 75, 77, 92-93, 111-12, 130
  load, 75, 76, 121-22
  schedule, 28, 39, 51, 57, 76, 103, 111, 121
  site, 12, 77, 78ff., 83-84, 88-99, 106, 110ff., 119, 120-21, 125, 127, 129-30
  space, 3, 38, 75, 77, 83ff., 110-11, 120-21, 129-30
Workflow, 83-84, 91-92
Workpaper, 9, 10-14, 18, 23, 126, 127
World-class status, xiv, 4, 7-8, 17, 23, 24, 26ff., 36ff., 50ff., 60ff., 68, 69ff. 80ff., 90ff., 117ff., 125ff., 131

Yankees
  League-Leader, kids' team, 5
  New York, 108-9